SPARK IT!

Mastering the Everyday
Art of Facilitating
Meaningful Interactions at
Work and in Life

Robert Radi, Ph.D.

INTEGRAL ADVANTAGE®
GAINING CLARITY IN COMPLEXITY

Copyright © 2025 by Robert Radi. Integral Advantage, Inc.

All rights reserved.

Published and Distributed in The United States of America by
Integral Advantage® Publishing Division.

www.integraladvantage.com

All rights reserved. No part of this book may be reproduced by any mechanical, photographic, or electronic process or in the form of a phonograph recording. Nor may it be stored in a retrieval system, transmitted, or otherwise be copied for public or private use, other than for "fair use" as brief quotations embodied in articles and reviews without prior written permission of the publisher. If you use any of the information in this book for yourself, which is your constitutional right, the author and the publisher assume no responsibility for your actions.

Library of Congress Control Number: 2025915021

Robert Radi

SPARK IT!

Business & Money › Skills › Communications
Personal Development › Relationships › Interpersonal Relations
Business & Money › Management & Leadership › Mentoring & Coaching

ISBN Paperback Book 979-8-9994214-0-1

ISBN Hard Cover 979-8-9994214-1-8

Integral Advantage® Publishing Division

Publisher's Note & Author DISCLAIMER

This book is intended to provide accurate and helpful information on the subject matter discussed. It is shared with the understanding that neither the author nor the publisher is providing psychological, medical, legal, or other professional services. The views expressed are those of the author and do not necessarily reflect the views of the publisher.
If you are in need of expert guidance or support, please seek help from a qualified professional. For urgent or crisis-related situations, contact a licensed provider or your local crisis hotline.

Contents

Introduction 5

Ch. 1 – SPARK IT! A Framework for Human-Centered Facilitation 11

Ch. 2 – Socratic Presence: Asking Over Telling 37

Ch. 3 – Facilitating Learning: Training or Development? 47

Ch. 4 – Crafting Your Facilitation Philosophy 61

Ch. 5 – Stories That Spark: Facilitating Meaning Through Narrative 71

Ch. 6 – The Courage to Adjust: Responsive Facilitation 87

Ch. 7 – Building the Emotional Infrastructure: Trust, Empathy, and Inclusive Dialogue 101

Ch. 8 – Engagement Design: Tools, Prompts, and Tactics .. 115

Ch. 9 – Virtual Doesn't Mean Distant 129

Ch. 10 – Facilitation as a Lifelong Practice 141

Conclusion 151

Acknowledgments 155

Bibliography 157

Index 165

About the Author 167

ROBERT RADI

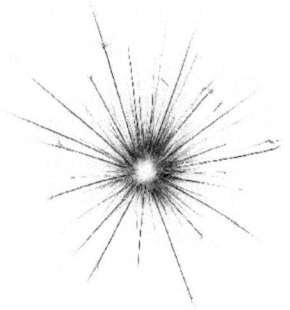

Dedication

To my wife, Charlotte, my son Max,
and my late mother, Rina.

I love you.

This book is dedicated to all those amazingly resilient individuals who find the courage to soldier through life's challenges and setbacks, making the odds against them irrelevant.

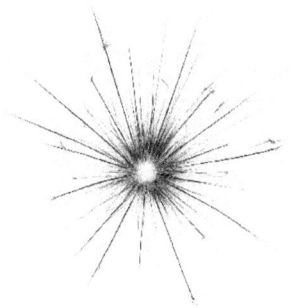

Introduction

The Everyday Art of Facilitation

It wasn't a keynote. There were no slides, breakout rooms, or a formal agenda. Just five people, a whiteboard, and the tension of an unsolved decision hanging in the air. The room had grown quiet after a flurry of back-and-forth. Everyone spoke. No one had aligned.

Then, a facilitator emerged. She didn't carry that title or role. She leaned in and asked a simple question:

"What's the real concern behind the concern?"

The room shifted. Postures relaxed. Heads turned. Someone exhaled. What followed wasn't magic. It was facilitation: unannounced, invisible, and deeply human.

We tend to think of facilitation as a practice reserved for off-site retreats, training sessions, or structured workshops. However, facilitation as a practice is not limited to sticky notes and whiteboards. It is not a title, a credential, or a line item on an agenda. At its heart, facilitation is an everyday art—an intentional way of being that creates the conditions for people to think more clearly, listen more deeply, and move forward more meaningfully.

Whether you're guiding a project team, navigating a challenging conversation with a colleague, coaching a direct report, or even discussing a family decision at the dinner table, you're facilitating. Or, more precisely, you have the opportunity to facilitate. And how you show up in those moments—what you notice, what you ask, what you hold back—can make the difference between confusion and clarity, frustration and connection, stagnation and progress.

We live in a world of constant conversation, but with surprisingly little meaningful dialogue. There is no shortage of words—meetings, emails, chat threads, debates—but too often, these exchanges feel transactional, rushed, or performative. People speak without being heard. Ideas circulate without being synthesized. Questions are asked without the curiosity to really listen for the answer. While two objects cannot occupy the same space simultaneously, two ideas from different perspectives can. It is called a dialogue. Hence, facilitation offers us a different path. It says: What if we made space for something new to emerge? What if we weren't here to convince, but to co-create?

That's what this book is about. *SPARK IT!* is not a manual for professional facilitators, though they are certainly welcome here. It is a guide for anyone who cares about the quality of their conversations and wants to turn ordinary moments into opportunities for insight, collaboration, and transformation. It is for managers, educators, coaches, parents, team leaders, and quiet catalysts—those who may not have the word "facilitator" in their job title but do the work of facilitating every single day.

Over time, I began to see that the best facilitators weren't those with the most polished delivery or the most tools in their toolkit. They were the ones who knew how to set a tone, guide inquiry, stay present to what was unfolding, and help others connect meaningfully with ideas, each other, and themselves. Their power wasn't in control; it was in how they cultivated conditions for learning, alignment, and momentum.

From that realization, I crafted the **SPARK IT!** framework—a compass to help navigate the complex and often messy terrain of human interaction. Each element reflects a principle that, when practiced, turns everyday interactions into facilitated experiences:

- **Set the Space** to establish clarity, trust, and purpose.
- **Prompt with Purpose** by asking questions that matter.
- **Anchor in Context** so that abstract ideas become relevant and real.
- **Respond with Curiosity** instead of judgment or reflex.
- **Kindle Connection** by building empathy and shared meaning.
- **Iterate in Real Time**, adapting to what's alive in the moment.
- **Translate Insight into Action**, so learning becomes movement.

This isn't a rigid model. It's not a checklist or a formula. **SPARK IT! is something you learn to feel as much as apply.** It helps you notice what's needed, what's missing, and what's possible when people come together to think, reflect, challenge, and build.

Before we explore each of these elements, it's worth pausing to consider the word 'facilitate' itself. The term comes from the Latin *facilis*, meaning "easy," which in turn derives from *facere* – "to make" or "to do." To facilitate, then, is not to direct, fix, or perform. It is, in its essence, to **make something easier**—to clear a path, soften the terrain, or remove friction so that others can move forward with greater freedom, clarity, and confidence.

That doesn't mean removing all difficulty. True facilitation isn't about simplification—it's about **clarification**. It's about helping people stay with the tension long enough to uncover what's real and valuable. A skilled facilitator does not carry people to the finish line—they illuminate the path, hold the space, and help others discover their own momentum.

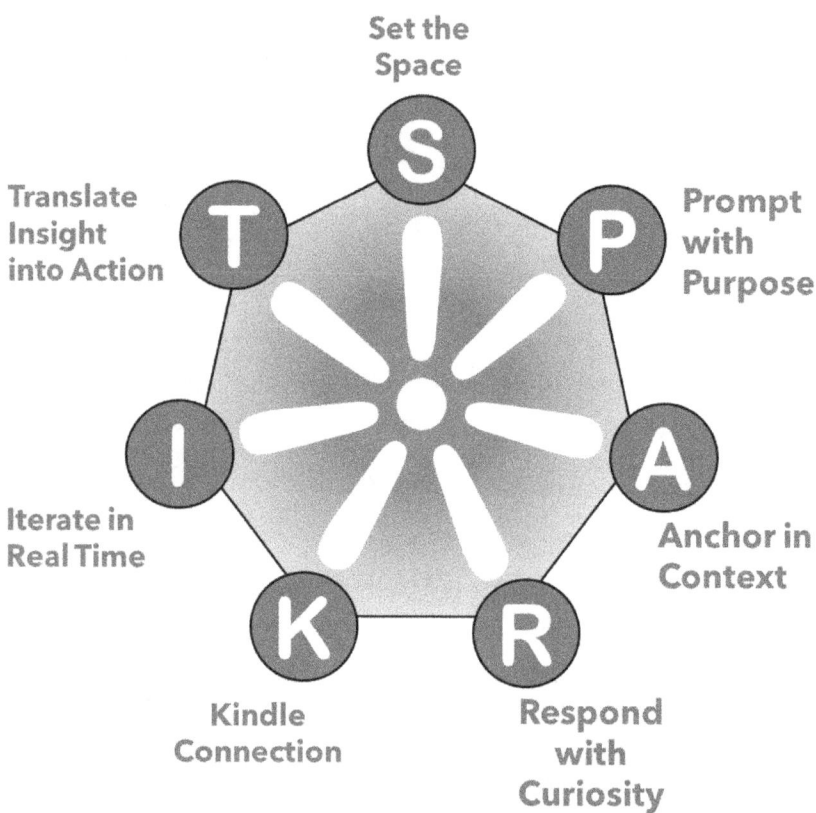

Image 1 - The **SPARK IT!** Framework

Throughout this book, we'll explore the SPARK IT! model in action, alongside stories, practices, and prompts designed to help you become more present, more attuned, and more effective in your interactions. More than anything, you'll learn to approach conversations—not just the formal ones, but the everyday ones—with a mindset of possibility. Because when we facilitate well, we don't just manage conversations; we facilitate meaningful connections. We **spark clarity, connection, and progress.**

You don't need a formal role to begin. You need a willingness to show up differently. To ask better questions. To hold space instead of filling it. To trust that there's wisdom in the room—even if it's not yet on the table.

So think back to a recent conversation that left you unsettled or stuck. Maybe it was a meeting where no decision was made. A complex dialogue that ended too quickly. A chance to help someone grow that turned into another tactical exchange. What if that wasn't a failure, but simply a missed opportunity to facilitate instead of fix?

This book is your invitation to reclaim those moments—to step into them with greater clarity, skill, and humanity.

Welcome to **SPARK IT!** Let's begin.

ROBERT RADI

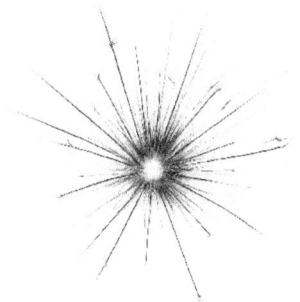

Chapter 1

SPARK IT! A Framework for Human-Centered Facilitation

A common misconception in facilitation is that success lies solely in structure. If the agenda is tight, the prompts are preloaded, the breakout rooms are assigned, and the slide deck is airtight, the group will align, engage, and deliver.

Then comes reality.

The group arrives, but someone's distracted. A voice dominates. Another one disappears—the energy shifts. The agenda feels suddenly rigid. The room doesn't match your prep—and now you're on. What do you do?

You facilitate, not from a script but from presence, attunement, and something more profound than logistics.

That "something" is what *SPARK IT!* was built to name, support, and practice.

The SPARK IT! model didn't emerge from theory alone. It came from years of facilitating in rooms and on screens of all kinds—boardrooms, classrooms, community gatherings, government teams, executive retreats, federal agencies, and quiet one-on-one coaching sessions. Different spaces. Different dynamics. Same underlying challenge:

"How do I help people move from where they are to where they need to go—together?"

This is a simple yet fundamental question, as it aligns with my definition of success. I am successful when I create and deliver value for others. That is how I measure my success.

What I learned is that the answer isn't about control. It's about conditions. Good facilitators don't force alignment. They create the **conditions** for emergence, understanding, and momentum. They understand that human conversations are fluid and that the role of the facilitator is to balance structure and softness simultaneously. To know when to guide, when to pause, when to ask, and when to let something land or hang.

This is where SPARK IT! comes in—not as a rigid method, but as a responsive, human-centered **facilitation compass**.

Let's walk through it.

S – Set the Space

Facilitation begins before a single word is spoken. It starts with how the space is shaped—physically, emotionally, and psychologically. Is this a place where people can speak honestly? Is uncertainty allowed here? Can disagreement surface without punishment or shame?

To *Set the Space* means more than arranging chairs or naming an agenda. It's about naming the purpose, establishing boundaries, and acknowledging what's at stake. It's about slowing the beginning to signal care and clarity. Nothing else will stick—no insight, no learning, no breakthrough—without a space that feels safe, clear, and intentional.

One team I worked with, preparing for a difficult reorganization, began their session not by jumping into problem-solving, but by going around the room and sharing one word that captured how they felt walking in. The honesty surprised them. It softened them. It made the work ahead possible.

Set the Space - Everyday Life Story:

The Dinner Table Check-In

Every evening, Mia, a single mother of two teenagers, noticed how their dinner conversations had become hollow, mostly heads down, phones out, with vague grunts between bites. One evening, instead of diving into the usual "How was your day?" script, she lit a candle, turned off the TV, and placed a sticky note at each setting with a simple handwritten question:

"What's something that made you think today?"

Initially, the responses were brief and cautious. But over time, this small ritual reshaped the space. Her kids began sharing more: random observations, quiet frustrations, and surprising joys. It wasn't therapy. It was a reset. The dining table became more than a place to eat—it became a space of attention, curiosity, and presence.

By shifting the emotional tone of the space, Mia didn't just encourage connection. She made it possible.

Set the Space - Everyday Work Story:

The Monday Morning Stand-Up That Changed Tone

At a marketing agency known for fast turnarounds and even faster meetings, the Monday morning stand-up was notoriously chaotic. People arrived late, multitasked openly, or avoided sharing blockers out of fear of looking weak.

One Monday, a team lead named Jose did something different. Before launching into updates, he asked everyone to pause, take a breath, and give a quick "weather report" on how they were feeling—sunny, cloudy, or stormy.

The shift was instant. One designer chuckled and said she felt "partly cloudy with a chance of coffee." Another quietly said, "stormy," and shared that she'd received hard personal news. No one rushed to fix anything. They simply acknowledged what was there. The space changed. People paid more attention. They listened better. They supported each other without being told to do so.

All because someone paused long enough to shape the tone, not just the tasks.

P – Prompt with Purpose

Facilitators aren't measured by what they say but by what they make possible—and what they make possible often begins not with answers, but with questions.

At its heart, facilitation is an act of inquiry. To Prompt with Purpose is to guide people toward discovery, rather than declaring outcomes. It's a subtle but profound shift—from giving direction to creating direction-finding moments. In this way, questions become tools of co-creation.

But not all questions are equal.

In our daily interactions, we often default to surface-level questions out of habit or politeness: "Everyone good?" "Any thoughts?" "Does that make sense?" These frequently shut people down rather than open them up. Worse, they put people on the spot without really offering them a space to reflect. There is a substantial difference between telling someone what we see (or what we perceive) and then asking them, "Do you see what I see?" versus asking them, "What do you see?" Seeking a conditioned response is not an effective method for inquiry.

Purposeful prompting goes deeper. It is clear, provocative, and anchored in genuine curiosity. The best prompts are not clever tricks or rhetorical moves; they are doorways into more profound meaning. They ask people to notice what they haven't yet noticed.

Questions like:

- "What's not being said right now that needs to be?"
- "If this went well, what would be different tomorrow?"
- "What part of this are we avoiding?"

These questions shift the air in a room. They stop the clock for a moment and make people think—not react.

The Philosophy of the Prompt

The word "prompt" comes from the Latin *promptus*, meaning "brought forth" or "made visible." To prompt, then, is to help something emerge—not to force it, but to make it possible. In ancient rhetorical traditions, the best orators weren't those who dazzled with speeches, but those who moved their audiences to think, reflect, and imagine. Socrates famously stated: "I cannot teach anything to anyone; all I can do is help them think."

A powerful question was seen as a moral tool, one that encouraged clarity, civic engagement, and moral reasoning. Today, we need that more than ever—in our workplaces, homes, classrooms, and communities.

The Neuroscience of a Good Question

Research in cognitive neuroscience reveals that questions activate brain regions associated with curiosity, learning, and emotional regulation. When we hear a meaningful question, especially one that's open-ended, our brain shifts into a different gear. Dopamine pathways associated with reward and exploration light up. This neurological engagement increases attention, memory retention, and willingness to collaborate.

In short: a well-crafted question doesn't just make someone think— it makes their brain *want* to think.

Prompt with Purpose - Everyday Life Story:

The Teenager and the Closed Door

Tina had tried every way to connect with her 16-year-old son, Marcus. He'd grown distant, retreating to his room, giving short answers, shrugging off conversation. One evening, instead of pushing for information, she sat beside him quietly and asked,

"What's something you wish I understood better about your world?"

There was a pause. A long one. Then, surprisingly, he answered:

"That I'm trying, even when it looks like I'm not."

That night didn't solve everything. But it unlocked something. A question—not a lecture, not a demand—had cracked the door open.

Often, it's about taking incremental steps, even if they don't feel like they're in the right direction. This movement can feel like a dance.

Ever tried to get a teenager to be consistent in executing a task? That is a dance characterized by three steps forward and two steps backward.

A few years ago, I was facilitating a course with the U.S. Air Force. Many participants were retired military now serving in civilian leadership roles—experts in their domains, with deep institutional knowledge and strong perspectives.

One of them, a leader overseeing cybersecurity, made a compelling comment during a discussion on complexity and interconnectedness. He said, "Everything is cybersecurity now. It affects every system and every process. Everyone has an opinion about it—even if they don't really understand it."

I nodded, then added with a smile, "You're absolutely right. I'm the father of a teenager who talks about cybersecurity every day—it's his passion. But somehow, he still forgets to lock the front door."

The whole cohort burst into laughter. It was a shared moment of recognition about the **challenges and opportunities of parenting**, as well as the needed humor that accompanies them.

Prompt with Purpose - Everyday Work Story:

The Meeting That Finally Mattered

During the monthly cross-functional meetings at a tech firm, the VP typically requested updates. Most people gave short, sanitized reports. Nothing ever felt urgent or revealing.

Then one month, she opened the meeting differently. She said:

"Before we dive in, let's each name one thing keeping us up at night about our team or our work."

At first, people hesitated. But someone broke the silence. Then another. Soon, the room filled not with updates but with truth. Concerns about burnout, lost alignment, and upcoming transitions. What followed wasn't chaos—but collaboration. People listened. They offered ideas. They committed to small changes.

All it took was one question with purpose.

Spotlight Story – What Question Should I Have Asked?

During my time serving on the La Quinta City Council, I had the opportunity to work with leaders from various sectors, including public, private, and community-based organizations. One of the most quietly impactful conversations I remember wasn't on a stage or in a speech. It happened in a small meeting room during a routine discussion about SilverRock, the city's municipal golf course.

At the time, Andy Vossler, CEO of Landmark Golf, was overseeing the management of the course. He was a contractor, yes—but more than that, a thoughtful partner in the city's stewardship of a public asset. Andy is the son of the late professional golfer and PGA Tour winner Ernie Vossler, so golf was in his DNA; however, his approach was distinctly his own.

Our meeting that day involved multiple parties: me, the city manager, and Andy. We covered a range of topics—from course operations to development timelines for nearby hotels. The agenda was packed. The tone was businesslike. The meeting could have ended like so many do—with a quick "thank you" and a shuffle of papers.

But instead, Andy paused and asked a question that has stayed with me for years:

"Was there a question I should have asked but didn't?"

That moment struck me, not as a performance, but as a genuine act of **humble leadership and facilitative awareness**. In one sentence, he created space for reflection, accountability, and trust. He signaled that his goal wasn't just to complete a checklist; it was to uncover anything **unspoken yet essential**.

This simple question exemplifies what it means to **prompt with purpose**. It reflects a mindset not of control, but of curiosity, not of transaction, but of contribution.

In facilitation, as in leadership, the best prompts aren't always the cleverest. They're the ones who **invite others to surface what matters**, especially when it hasn't yet been said.

A - Anchor in Context

Facilitation can't float above reality in an esoteric fashion. It must be grounded in the environment, stakes, and lived experience of those involved. This is what I mean by **Anchor in Context**. I often joke with participants in my courses that if I had to pay one dollar for every time I use the word *context*, I would be broke! Indeed, it is one of my favorite words and for good reasons.

Context gives meaning. Without it, even the most well-intentioned conversation risks drifting into abstraction or irrelevance. In other words, context ensures that we don't go down the proverbial rabbit hole. People don't engage with ideas in isolation; they engage with how those ideas relate to their lives, their work, their struggles, and their hopes. Anchoring means connecting the abstract to the actual or tangible.

It means resisting the temptation to lead with theory or templates, and instead starting with what's alive:

- What pressures are people facing?
- What historical patterns shape the present moment?

- What personal experiences are influencing how people show up today?

To anchor is not to restrict—it's to stabilize. Just as a ship needs an anchor to remain steady in shifting waters, people need shared reference points to feel oriented and purposeful in complex conversations.

When I facilitate professional environments, I begin building the learning community by making a clear statement about context. I tell the participants that we will create the learning experience together, and for that, I will bring the content, and they will bring the context. The context in which they operate is often individually unique, even when they all work for the same agency or organization. So, context matters.

Why Context Is More Than Background

In the ancient Greek tradition, context—*Kairos* was seen as the "right or opportune moment" to act. It wasn't just *when* something happened, but *why* that moment mattered. The power of facilitation often lies in sensing Kairos—understanding not only the content of the discussion but also the undercurrents shaping it.

In storytelling, context provides setting, mood, and significance. In neuroscience, context shapes perception itself: our brains interpret new information based on prior experience and environmental cues. Without context, even the most basic facts can feel disconnected or confusing.

Facilitators who ignore context risk unintentionally excluding people or misreading the room. Those who honor it build trust, relevance, and real possibility.

Anchor in Context – Everyday Life Story:

The Birthday That Wasn't About Cake

Nora's father had just passed away, and her daughter's birthday was approaching. Everyone in the family was trying to keep things "normal," pushing through with party plans. But something felt off, forced, and hollow.

The morning of the celebration, Nora sat with her daughter and said, "I know we're supposed to be excited today, and we *are*, but I also know there's a sadness in the air. How are you feeling, really?"

Her daughter teared up and whispered, "I miss Grandpa. I wanted him to be here."

They lit a candle in his memory during the party. It didn't make the grief disappear, but it made space for it. The celebration became more honest—more whole.

That's what anchoring looks like. Not just pressing forward, but pausing long enough to ask: *What's the real context we're in? What is the context in which we operate?*

Anchor in Context – Everyday Work Story:

The Training That Finally Worked

A federal agency launched a new change management training for its regional managers. The first few sessions flopped. Attendance was poor. Feedback said it was "detached" and "not relevant."

Then one facilitator, Maya, did something transformative but straightforward. She opened the next session by asking, "What's one real challenge you're facing this week that this training *has to* help you with?"

The room shifted. People spoke about hiring freezes, staff burnout, and inconsistent directives from HQ. Maya listened, took notes, and reworked her examples on the fly, connecting every framework she introduced to a challenge someone had named.

That session was rated the highest of the series.

Maya didn't change the material. She altered the anchoring.

R - Respond with Curiosity

When people speak, they aren't just sharing information—they're revealing their inner world: their concerns, their questions, their interpretations of what matters. In moments like these, the facilitator's response can either widen the conversation or shut it down. That's why **Respond with Curiosity** is a critical act of leadership.

Curiosity is not neutral; it's an intentional posture. It means choosing wonderment over assumption, openness over control, and interest over defensiveness. It doesn't mean agreement. It means the willingness to understand before deciding what to do.

A curious facilitator leans in. Not with "gotcha" questions or faux empathy, but with genuine interest:

- "What's leading you to see it that way?"
- "Can you say more about what's underneath that concern?"
- "That's a different take—what shaped it for you?"

These responses signal something powerful: *You matter. What you say has weight. And there's space for your thinking here.*

Why Curiosity Is a Cognitive Superpower

Neuroscience shows that curiosity activates the brain's reward system. When we're curious, we become more engaged, more open to learning, and more connected to others. Curiosity literally primes the brain for exploration; it helps us notice more, remember more, and judge less.

From a philosophical lens, curiosity was a cornerstone of Socratic dialogue. Socrates believed that wisdom wasn't about having answers but about asking the right questions. His method—responding not with rebuttals but with deeper inquiry—reflected the belief that truth emerges through shared exploration, not personal assertion.

In facilitation, curiosity keeps us agile. It slows down the impulse to fix, judge, or pivot too quickly. It allows the conversation to go where it needs to go, not just where we planned.

Respond with Curiosity - Everyday Life Story:

The Piano Practice Breakdown

Elena's son, Jonah, had been dragging his feet with piano practice. One night, after another long standoff, she caught herself about to snap. Instead, she paused and said, "You used to love playing. What's making it hard lately?"

Jonah shrugged. "It's not fun anymore. It feels like homework."

They talked. It turned out the new pieces were too hard, and he was embarrassed to admit it. They picked a few simpler songs that night. He played them with joy.

The breakthrough didn't come from pushing harder; it came from *curiosity*. That simple shift restored connection and momentum.

Respond with Curiosity - Everyday Work Story:

The "Difficult" Colleague

Amira was leading a cross-functional project. One stakeholder, Greg, was constantly resistant—questioning timelines, pushing back on deliverables, and sounding, frankly, combative.

In a side conversation, Amira chose a different tack. "I notice you've raised concerns in every meeting. What's at stake for you in this project that maybe we haven't talked about yet?"

Greg paused. Then he admitted: if the timeline slipped, his team's budget would be cut. He wasn't being difficult—he was under pressure.

From that point forward, the tone changed. They built safeguards together. Greg became one of the project's biggest supporters.

Curiosity didn't just diffuse tension—it built trust.

K - Kindle Connection

Facilitation is not just about guiding a process—it's about *igniting human connection*. Without it, even the best-designed conversations fall flat. People might show up, speak up, even nod along—but they won't *lean in*, they won't stretch, and they won't grow. Why? Because growth happens in relationships.

To Kindle Connection is to create the conditions where people feel valued, heard, respected, and part of something larger than themselves. It's the spark that turns a roomful of individuals into a collective with shared energy and purpose.

This doesn't happen by accident. It happens through intentional moments of empathy, recognition, and shared vulnerability.

Why Connection Is Fundamental

From a neuroscience perspective, we're wired for connection. Oxytocin–sometimes called the "trust hormone"–is released through shared eye contact, laughter, affirmation, and empathy. It softens defensiveness, increases openness, and fosters the kind of safety that encourages people to take risks.

Historically, rituals of connection have anchored human communities–from indigenous talking circles to the storytelling traditions of every culture. Connection is what made collaboration possible long before we had Zoom links and Gantt charts.

In facilitation, connection enables the exploration of complexity. When people trust each other, they don't need to agree–they need to understand and respect each other's place in the system. Connection makes disagreement productive. It builds resilience in the room.

Ways to Kindle Connection

- **Acknowledge effort, not just outcomes.** People want to know their contributions matter, even if the work is unfinished.

- **Use people's names.** It's simple, but powerful. It humanizes.

- **Pause for appreciation.** Ask, "Who helped you think differently today?"

- **Reflect back emotional tone.** "I'm sensing some hesitation–does that feel right to name?"

These small gestures often unlock disproportionate results. They transform cold rooms into live rooms.

Kindle Connection – Everyday Life Story:

The Power of a Sticky Note

Raj was a software engineer working late nights. His daughter, Ava, started slipping notes under his home office door—little drawings, jokes, even a stick figure comic strip about "Super Dad."

Raj began taping them to his monitor.

One day, he replied with a sticky note of his own: "Thanks for the smiles. Want to get ice cream after school?"

The notes became their thing. No grand gestures. Just consistency. Just *presence*.

The connection didn't require hours. It required *attention*.

Kindle Connection – Everyday Work Story:

A Gratitude Loop

During a high-stakes product launch, a project manager named Lila invited her team to close each day's stand-up with one sentence: "Something I appreciated about someone today was…"

At first, it felt awkward. But within a week, people were naming things like "Thanks to Marcus for fixing that bug at 9 p.m." and "Shoutout to Chloe for calming a nervous client."

The tone of the meetings shifted. Frustrations still happened, but people gave each other more grace. They assumed good intent. They felt like a team.

Connection wasn't the *extra* work. It was the *real* work that made everything else possible.

I - Iterate in Real Time

Facilitation isn't a static script—it's a living, breathing engagement. To facilitate well is to listen deeply, watch closely, and *adapt in motion*. The best facilitators don't just *follow* the plan; they *respond* to what's alive in the room.

To Iterate in Real Time is to treat the agenda not as a checklist, but as a hypothesis. A facilitator's real skill is evident when something unexpected arises—tension, laughter, silence, or resistance—and they respond with presence, not panic.

It's about staying open to emergence without losing direction.

The Science Behind Flexibility

Cognitive neuroscience tells us that adaptability relies on the brain's *prefrontal cortex*, which is responsible for our executive function. The term **"executive function"** was first coined by **Adele Diamond**, a pioneering developmental cognitive neuroscientist. She used the term to describe a set of cognitive processes—such as working memory, cognitive flexibility, and inhibitory control—that enable people to plan, focus attention, follow instructions, and manage multiple tasks effectively.

While earlier psychologists, such as Luria and Lezak, contributed to the foundational understanding of frontal lobe functions, it was Adele Diamond who formally introduced the concept of executive function into developmental and neuroscience discourse, emphasizing its early development in children and its crucial role in learning, behavior, and emotional regulation.

When facilitators stay grounded and open, they're more able to regulate emotion, reframe in the moment, and make better decisions under stress. Conversely, when facilitators become rigid or reactive, the brain shifts into defensive mode, narrowing perception and reducing creativity.

Iterating in real time is also a relational signal. It shows people that their contributions matter enough to shape the process. That *they* are co-authors of what unfolds, not just passengers on someone else's ride.

Iteration in Practice

- When a conversation goes deeper than planned, let it—if it's where energy and insight are.
- If a group doesn't respond to a prompt, don't blame the group. Rethink the prompt.
- Notice nonverbal cues: glazed eyes, leaning in, crossed arms. Adjust accordingly.
- Be willing to name what's happening in the room. "I'm sensing we may be pushing ahead before we're ready. Should we pause?"

Facilitators who iterate competently often say things like:

- "Let's check in. Does this still feel like the right focus?"
- "We had planned to do X, but I'm hearing that Y may be more useful. Thoughts?"
- "It seems like this is striking a chord. Should we stay with it?"

Iteration doesn't mean improvising without aim. It means being agile *with intention*.

Iterate in Real Time – Everyday Life Story:

The Re-Routed Road Trip

Jess and Jordan had a weekend getaway planned—driving up the coast, checking off their carefully mapped itinerary of beaches and cafes. But halfway through, road closures rerouted them inland. Frustrated, they pulled over to regroup.

Jordan suggested they stop at a small town they'd never heard of. One antique store, one hidden waterfall, and one spontaneous hike later, they agreed it was the best part of the trip.

The trip's magic wasn't in the plan. It was in their *willingness to depart from it.*

Iterate in Real Time – Everyday Work Story:

The Unscripted Staff Retreat

During a nonprofit's annual staff retreat, the leadership team had prepared a full agenda of strategic planning sessions. However, after the opening icebreaker, someone shared that the team had felt disconnected since transitioning to a hybrid setup. Heads nodded. Faces softened.

Instead of diving into planning, the facilitator paused and asked, "Would it serve us better to spend this morning reconnecting before we plan for the year ahead?"

They shifted the agenda and began sharing stories, acknowledging tensions, and laughing together. Later, the strategic work came more easily. More aligned. More real.

The facilitator didn't lose the plot—they *earned the trust to rewrite it.*

T – Translate Insight into Action

Insight alone is never enough. A spark is beautiful—but without fuel or forward motion, it flickers out. Facilitation, at its most impactful, turns reflection into movement. It translates the "aha" into "what now?"

In group settings, people often reach meaningful realizations. They voice clarity, uncover assumptions, and connect ideas that had previously lived in isolation. However, unless these insights are anchored in next steps—such as behaviors, agreements, or experiments—they risk dissolving as soon as the session ends.

Facilitators help bridge that gap.

This isn't about pushing for premature decisions or drafting rigid plans. It's about asking: *How will what we've uncovered today inform what happens tomorrow?*

The facilitator becomes a translator, not of one language into another, but of understanding into application, and of application into implementation. That translation appears differently depending on the context. Sometimes it means:

- **Naming the shift.** "What changed for you in this conversation?"
- **Anchoring learning.** "What's one thing you want to remember from today?"
- **Defining action.** "What's a first step that feels both possible and meaningful?"
- **Creating accountability.** "Who needs to hear this beyond this room?"

Good facilitation makes sure momentum doesn't die in the room—

it follows people out the door.

Translate Insight into Action - Everyday Life Story

From Resolution to Routine

Riley and Taylor, who lived together, often found themselves having the same argument about the state of the kitchen after meals. After one long, honest conversation, they both finally understood the underlying issue wasn't just about chores—it was about feeling respected.

The insight was powerful, even emotional. But the next night, the dishes still piled up. The moment of clarity had created no real change.

So they paused again, and this time, translated the insight into action. They set a timer for ten minutes after dinner: both would clean together—music on, no excuses. It wasn't about perfection. It was about showing up for each other in a shared ritual.

What changed their relationship wasn't just the talking—it was the turning of understanding into something lived.

Translate Insight into Action - Everyday Work Story

From Post-Mortem to Prototyping

At the end of a significant product launch, a cross-functional tech team gathered for a post-mortem. The discussion was rich—vulnerabilities surfaced, tensions were named, and lessons were learned. It could have ended there.

But the facilitator paused and asked, "Which of these learnings should we prototype into our next sprint?"

The room shifted. People got specific. One engineer proposed a 10-minute "risk round" at the start of each planning meeting, and a designer committed to documenting edge-case scenarios on a weekly basis. Suddenly, insights had traction.

Six weeks later, those simple changes had become team norms. Not because the conversation was brilliant, but because someone ensured the learning moved from idea to iteration.

The Takeaway

Insight is fragile. Without translation, it evaporates.

Facilitators play a crucial role not only in helping people see, but also in helping them decide how to apply what they now see to their actions.

Translating Insight to Action isn't the end of facilitation; it's what makes everything else stick.

Putting It All Together

What SPARK IT! offers is not a script. It's a posture. A practice. A compass.

Each of its seven elements is deceptively simple, but together, they form a dynamic approach for navigating moments of connection, decision, tension, and learning in any setting:

- You **Set the Space** when you pause before reacting, or invite someone in rather than pushing them away.

- You **Prompt with Purpose** when you ask a question that opens—not closes—a conversation.

- You **Anchor in Context** when you help others see how this moment connects to the bigger picture.

- You **Respond with Curiosity** when you choose listening over labeling.

- You **Kindle Connection** when you foster empathy instead of control.

- You **Iterate in Real Time** when you adapt instead of insisting on your plan.

- And you **Translate Insight to Action** when you turn reflection into meaningful follow-through.

Each of these practices is valuable in its own right. But together, they spark the kind of presence that makes others feel valued, heard, and willing to engage.

Whether you're leading a team meeting, parenting through a meltdown, mentoring a colleague, or navigating conflict with a friend, facilitation shows up as a generous force. It's not about control. It's about creating the conditions where growth, change, and connection can happen.

You don't need a title to be a facilitator. You just need to believe that people are worth the effort—and that better conversations lead to better outcomes.

SPARK IT! as Everyday Leadership

These seven elements don't always occur in order. They're not a checklist or recipe—they're a rhythm. A way of moving with intention through human interaction. Together, they help you cultivate the presence and awareness needed to facilitate at any level, in any context.

In high-stakes meetings, SPARK IT! helps surface what's unspoken and unblock what's stuck. In quiet one-on-ones, it allows participants to think more clearly than they have in weeks. In everyday conversations, it becomes a habit—a way of being present with more purpose and less performance.

This model isn't meant to elevate you as the center of attention. It's meant to make you a center of gravity. Someone who guides with presence, not pressure. With design, not dominance. Someone who creates the conditions for clarity, trust, and momentum—without needing to take the credit.

You don't need to memorize SPARK IT! You already embody parts of it. The work ahead is to notice. Notice where it naturally appears in your practice. Notice where you resist. Notice what comes alive when you shift your approach.

- Do you tend to leap into action before setting the space?
- Do you rely on content instead of context?
- Are your questions truly opening the room—or closing it?

None of this is about perfection. Facilitation is a practice of intentional imperfection. Of tuning into what's needed, holding space long enough for others to see what they didn't know they needed—and offering just enough light to move toward it.

So let's begin. Not with control, but with curiosity. Not with the goal of mastering others, but of deepening your presence.

What will you spark next?

Chapter 1 in a Nutshell:
In Life & At Work

In Life:

The SPARK IT framework isn't just for professional facilitators—it's a mindset you can bring into daily interactions. At home, start by setting the space with intention: a clear tone, a moment of pause, or simply your full presence. Prompt with questions that matter, listen without rushing to solve them, and respond with genuine curiosity. Whether you're navigating a challenging conversation or planning a family decision, anchoring in shared purpose builds connection and trust. Even small exchanges—done with clarity, openness, and adaptability—can become moments of meaningful facilitation.

At Work:

Effective facilitation isn't about being the loudest voice in the room; it's about being the clearest. Use SPARK IT! to guide team meetings, project kickoffs, or leadership conversations. Set the space by defining purpose and expectations. Prompt with questions that invite insight, not just status updates. Anchor abstract goals in the team's context. Respond with curiosity to unexpected input. Kindle genuine connection, iterate when things shift, and always close with action steps that carry the conversation forward. Facilitation becomes your leadership tool—not a separate role, but a strategic posture.

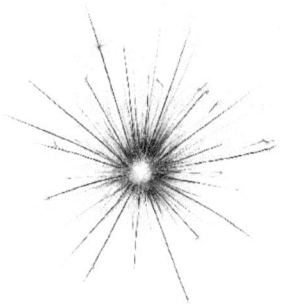

Chapter 2

Socratic Presence: Asking Over Telling

The question has a quiet power that doesn't seek a conclusion but a deeper understanding.

In one of the first leadership retreats I facilitated, a participant asked a direct question:

"So what's the right way to motivate a disengaged team?"

I paused. I could have listed some research-backed strategies or shared a story from experience. But instead, I said:

"What do you already know about what's draining their motivation?"

The question bounced back to him, and opened something up not just for him, but for the whole group. His assumptions surfaced. The room leaned in. A richer dialogue unfolded. He found his own answer—not because I told him, but because I didn't.

I spend more time developing my presentation decks than I am willing to admit to myself or others. Inviting, engaging, and visually appealing. Yet, that moment didn't require a PowerPoint slide. It required a mindset: what I've come to call **Socratic presence**.

The Shift from Answering to Facilitating Thinking

Socratic presence is rooted in a truth that often feels uncomfortable in high-achieving environments: **you don't have to have the answer.** Your value as a facilitator isn't in what you say, it's in what you help others discover.

Named after Socrates, the Greek philosopher who claimed to know nothing but pursued wisdom through questions, the Socratic method lives at the heart of effective facilitation. It's not just a technique. It's a way of being—one that replaces instruction with inquiry and creates learning through discovery.

In facilitation, Socratic presence means holding space for:

- Inquiry over instruction
- Dialogue over debate
- Curiosity over control
- Exploration over explanation

When you lead with answers, you risk creating dependence. When you lead with questions, you **build capacity**.

A Brief Journey to the Agora: Socrates and the Method That Bears His Name

To understand why we speak of *Socratic presence* and the *Socratic method*, we need to travel back to ancient Athens, nearly 2,500 years ago.

Socrates, a stonemason by trade and a philosopher by practice, never wrote a book. He left no scrolls, no self-authored doctrine. What we know of him comes primarily from his students—most famously Plato, who made Socrates the central voice in his philosophical dialogues. In those texts, Socrates doesn't lecture. He questions. Gently, persistently, and often uncomfortably.

What made Socrates radical for his time—and why his approach remains foundational to education, law, leadership, and facilitation—is that he refused to accept ideas at face value. He didn't seek to win arguments. He sought to illuminate assumptions. His method was simple: **ask questions that reveal contradictions, test definitions, and invite people to reexamine what they think they know.**

This dialectical process, later formalized as the *Socratic Method*, is not a technique for interrogation. It is a disciplined practice of inquiry—an act of mutual discovery. Socrates believed that wisdom was not something one person handed to another, but something that emerged when we rigorously, humbly, and communally examined our thinking.

The method was not always popular. In fact, Socrates was put on trial for "corrupting the youth" and "impiety," primarily because he challenged the intellectual arrogance of Athens' elites. He chose to drink hemlock rather than renounce his commitment to questioning and inquiry. His legacy, however, has endured. Centuries later, his method remains a gold standard of learning through dialogue—and a quiet act of civic courage.

Why It Matters in Facilitation

Socratic presence is not about mimicking an ancient philosopher. It's about embracing a deeper posture—one that says:

"I'm not here to lecture. I'm here to think with you."

Whether in a conference room or a classroom, effective facilitators are heirs to this tradition. They hold space for complexity. They model humility. And they help others examine their beliefs without stripping away their dignity.

When we ask purposeful, clarifying, and open-ended questions, we are not just managing conversation—we're practicing a kind of modern-day philosophy: helping people learn how to learn, not what to think.

And that is the heart of facilitation.

What Socratic Presence Looks Like in Practice

It's tempting to imagine that a good facilitator must be a master orator—articulate, always prepared, a smooth deliverer of content. But more often, facilitation is about resisting that temptation. It's about tuning your internal antenna to the group's energy and responding—not with content, but with curiosity.

It sounds like:

- "What do you make of that?"
- "What's the tension you're sensing underneath that idea?"
- "Who's seeing it differently?"
- "What are we assuming here?"
- "If this were easy, what would we be doing already?"

Sometimes it's as simple as, "Tell me more." Those three words—delivered sincerely—can unlock more insight than a thirty-minute lecture.

Socratic presence also means knowing when to **hold the silence** after a question. The instinct to fill silence is strong—especially when the room gets tense. But some of the most transformational facilitation moments happen when the question is allowed to breathe. Decanting like a robust red wine. Silence is where thinking deepens. Where the unsaid starts to form. Your comfort with silence models safety.

Balancing Inquiry and Guidance

Of course, Socratic presence doesn't mean abdicating all direction. Facilitation isn't an endless open circle of inquiry. There's still structure, timing, and goals. But the presence you bring to that structure—the restraint you exercise in not rushing to solve—creates the space for participants to arrive at something more meaningful than what you could have delivered.

Think of it this way: when people find their insight, they **own it**. When we spoon-feed them, they often admire the presentation but forget the message.

Socratic presence says, "You're capable of reaching this, and I'm here to help you navigate it, not to deliver it for you."

The Discipline of Not Knowing

This posture isn't always easy, especially for those of us trained to be experts, fixers, or leaders. Not knowing can feel like weakness. But in facilitation, it is a strength. It is the ground from which authentic connection grows.

To stand in front of a room and choose curiosity over certainty takes discipline. But it also liberates you. You don't have to have the solution. You simply have to keep the dialogue alive, clear, and purposeful.

Participants don't need us to be all-knowing. They need us to help them make sense of their own knowing.

Facilitator Reflection: How Curious Am I Really?

To cultivate Socratic presence, begin by asking yourself:

- Do I rush to fix, or do I linger in inquiry?
- Do I default to answers when I feel the energy dip?
- Can I stay grounded when a question doesn't land right away?
- Do I make room for alternative views, or subtly steer people to my frame?
- What kind of questions do I tend to ask? Information-seeking? Perspective-expanding? Provocative?

One of the most courageous acts in facilitation is to stay curious just a few seconds longer than is comfortable.

Practice: Reshaping the Question

Take five questions you commonly ask in your facilitation or leadership conversations. Now reframe each to:

- Make it more open-ended
- Invite reflection or perspective
- Assume the answer lies within the group

For example:

Instead of "Does everyone agree?" → try "What's one thing we might be missing here?"
Instead of "What do you think the solution is?" → try "What's the tension we need to name before jumping to a fix?"

This is how inquiry becomes design—and how facilitation becomes presence.

The Quiet Authority of Inquiry

People sometimes ask, "But doesn't asking too many questions make me seem uncertain?"

My answer: It doesn't make you less certain. It makes you **more powerful because you're making space for others to think.**
The strongest facilitators don't dominate. They **draw out**. They don't use questions to trap or test, but to open and expand. They make others feel capable, valued, and responsible for their part in the collective work.

Socratic presence doesn't mean staying passive. It means being precise and intentional with your curiosity. It means making space not just for people to speak, but for them to think.

And in a world that constantly rushes us to act, that pause—the one created by a well-placed, open-hearted question—might be the most radical contribution you can make.

Bridging Socrates and SPARK IT!

Socrates taught us that learning begins not with instruction but with inquiry. His method wasn't about providing the correct answers—it was about asking the right questions to unlock deeper thinking. In that sense, Socrates was an early facilitator, setting the space for rigorous dialogue, prompting with purpose, and kindling the kind of connections that carried far beyond a single conversation.

This spirit lives at the core of the SPARK IT! framework.

Each element of SPARK IT – from **Setting the Space** to **Prompting with Purpose**, from **Responding with Curiosity** to **Translating Insight to Action**—mirrors the intentionality behind the Socratic tradition. But unlike the singular figure of the philosopher, SPARK IT! invites anyone to become a steward of meaningful interaction.

Where Socrates relied on one-on-one dialogue, today's facilitators often work within groups, teams, and complex systems. SPARK IT! adapts that ancient impulse to today's contexts. It's less about leading people to a single truth and more about opening space where multiple truths can be examined, challenged, and refined.

While the Socratic Method provided the seed, SPARK IT! offers a system—a flexible, human-centered approach to helping others think, connect, and grow. In the chapters ahead, we'll explore how each piece builds the muscle of modern facilitation and how you can carry that lineage forward, one purposeful question at a time.

Chapter 2 in a Nutshell:
In Life & At Work

In Life:

Socratic Presence isn't reserved for classrooms or philosophical debates—it's a mindset we can carry into everyday life. When we ask before telling, we build trust, deepen relationships, and cultivate curiosity in ourselves and others. Whether you're parenting, navigating friendships, or mentoring someone, thoughtful inquiry opens space for connection and discovery. Practice replacing advice with genuine questions, such as, *"What do you think is the next best step?"* to invite ownership and reflection.

At Work:

In professional settings, Socratic Presence shifts us from being solution-pushers to possibility-guides. It empowers colleagues, energizes teams, and fosters learning cultures. Start meetings with open-ended prompts, use inquiry to navigate conflict, and resist the urge to fill silence with answers. By asking better questions—especially ones that reveal assumptions or challenge the status quo—you become a facilitative leader who doesn't just transmit knowledge, but transforms thinking.

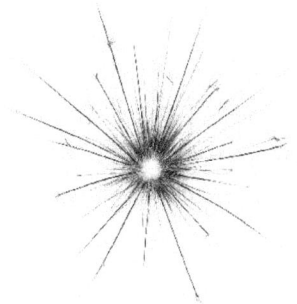

Chapter 3

Facilitating Learning: Training or Development?

In one of the early sessions I facilitated for a group of new managers, a participant raised her hand halfway through the morning and said, "I'm not sure what we're supposed to be learning. No one's told us the right answers yet."

I smiled, gently, and replied, "That's because I'm not here to give you answers. I'm here to help you discover the answers that work in your world."

She blinked—politely, confused. But by the end of the day, she came up and said, "You made us do the thinking. That was… different. It stuck." We both laughed.

It stuck because she wasn't just trained—she began to develop.

And that distinction matters. When we **Anchor in Context**, we help others connect the moment to something bigger, nudging them to think beyond the task to the meaning. In everyday interactions, whether we're managing a team, mentoring a peer, or engaging our youth, there are opportunities to go beyond explanation and into transformation. We do this by widening the cognitive aperture.

This is where Bloom's Cognitive Taxonomy offers a helpful perspective. The lower three levels – **Remembering**, **Understanding**, and **Applying** – are often the domain of training. These levels are about retention, clarity, and execution. They're linear, measurable, and necessary when precision matters. But facilitation stands higher, a cut above.

The upper levels – **Analyzing**, **Evaluating**, and **Creating** – invite complexity in thinking. This is the space of development. They don't ask for the "right" answer, but for better questions, deeper insight, and contextual judgment. These levels aren't achieved through lectures; they require reflection, dialogue, and meaning-making. They need us to hold space for uncertainty long enough for real understanding to emerge.

When we facilitate, we're not just transferring knowledge; we're fostering the ability to think critically about thinking. That's the move from training to development. From content delivery to capacity building. From information to transformation.

The Mistaken Identity: Training Disguised as Facilitation

In organizational life, we often conflate **training** with **development**, and as a result, we confuse **instructing** with **facilitating**.

Training, at its core, is about **transferring knowledge or skills**. It's often standardized, structured, and transactional. It answers questions like:

- How do I complete this task?
- What are the steps in this process?
- What's the protocol?

There's absolutely nothing wrong with training. In fact, it's essential in environments that require precision, compliance, or procedural mastery, such as onboarding, safety certification, and software tutorials. In those contexts, clarity and repetition are strengths.

However, when we approach leadership, team dynamics, emotional intelligence, or culture-building as if they can be "trained" in the same way, we run into trouble. Because those areas aren't about *correct answers*, they're about *complex human thinking and behavior*. They require reflection, dialogue, ownership, and experimentation. This holds true in both our professional and personal lives.

That's where **development** enters.

Development Is a Different Game

Development is not about only passing down information; it's about creating a new understanding. It's about **supporting transformation**. It's slower. Messier. More personal. It works not only by instruction, but by insight. And it sticks because the learner becomes the builder. Concepts are contextualized and become implementable.

Facilitation is the engine of development. It doesn't start from "What should I tell them?" but from "What do they need space to explore?"

Development asks:

- What's shaping your current thinking?

- What patterns are you repeating—and why?
- What might it take for you to grow into your next version of yourself?

In this work, the facilitator isn't a teller. They're a **midwife of meaning**—helping people give birth to their own learning.

What's at Stake When We Confuse the Two?

When we treat development like training, we reduce people to passive recipients. We overload sessions with slides, cram too many models into tight timelines, and leave no room for contextualization or dialogue. Learners walk away with notebooks full of someone else's framework but little clarity on what they actually believe or will do differently.

But when we treat development with the care it deserves—when we **facilitate, not dictate**—people leave with insight. With agency. With renewed self-awareness and practical traction.

They may not be able to recite every theory you shared. But they will remember the moment something clicked. And that moment is the seed of change.

The Role of the Facilitator in Development

The facilitator in a developmental space wears a different lens. Instead of seeing the room as a set of empty vessels to be filled, they see it as a landscape of lived experience waiting to be activated.

That means:

- Asking more than explaining
- Guiding reflection more than delivering content

- Surfacing lived wisdom rather than importing expertise
- Creating structure without constriction
- Using tools not as crutches, but as invitations to think

Facilitators **don't tell people what to see**. They help people see what they're looking at in a different light and reframe it from a different angle. Once they see it, they cannot unsee it, and that alone is key to **Translating Insight into Action.**

We are not instructors. We are **constructive provocateurs**. We challenge with care, reveal with empathy, and move at the speed of trust.

Why This Matters in a Permanently Complex World

We no longer live in an era where mastery of static knowledge guarantees success. The challenges leaders and teams face today are fluid, cross-disciplinary, emotionally charged, and often without precedent. No single model or manual holds the solution. We live in the "yes, and . . . " era.

In this world, the most valuable skill is the ability to **learn, unlearn, and relearn in context**. And that doesn't happen through training alone. It occurs when people are given the space to grapple with nuance, reflect on their impact, and integrate learning into their identity.

That's the space facilitators hold.

What Developmental Facilitation Sounds Like

Here's how facilitation shifts when you move from training to development:

Training Prompt	Developmental Prompt
"Here are the four steps to follow."	"Which step would feel most natural for you? Which one would challenge you?"
"Does everyone understand the model?"	"What part of this model affirms what you've already experienced?"
"This is how high-performing teams work."	"Where does your team already reflect this? Where does it diverge—and why?"

Notice the differences? The content still matters in development, but the **participant's meaning-making** takes center stage.

Facilitator Self-Check: Training vs. Development

Before a session, ask yourself:

- Am I designing for retention or reflection?
- Are my goals about clarity or transformation, or both?
- Where do participants make meaning in the session, not just receive it?
- How am I structuring time for them to try on ideas, not just hear them?

- What mindset am I bringing: instructor, consultant, coach… or facilitator?

The answers will help you shift your stance and shape your structure, and act with clarity in your role, enabling you to **Kindle Connections** and **Iterate in Real Time**.

From Informing to Inviting

To facilitate is to trust. To believe that people can generate wisdom, not just absorb it. That's a risk—and a gift. You're not creating followers. You're cultivating thinkers.

And in a world that often treats learning like consumption, your choice to facilitate—to develop, not just train—is a quiet act of rebellion. A signal that we are not just here to **deliver content**, but to **develop capacity**.

Because the best sessions don't end when the workshop closes. They echo. They ripple. They change how people see and behave the next day—and the day after that.

That is the power of developmental facilitation. And that is the heart of your role.

A few years ago, I was asked to lead a workshop on "accountability." The client—a well-meaning executive—wanted me to train his managers on how to "hold people's feet to the fire." He sent me bullet points. He expected a slide deck. He envisioned me standing at the front of the room, running through a framework on how to correct behavior, document issues, and enforce compliance.

Instead, I opened the session with a single prompt:

"Tell me about a time you avoided holding someone accountable. What stopped you?"

The room went silent. And then the stories started. Not about systems or checklists—but about fear. About relationships. About the cost of confrontation. One manager said, "I didn't want to risk losing him. He has been with us ten years." Another admitted, "I just don't know how to bring things up without sounding like I'm scolding someone."

By the time we introduced any methodology or techniques, we had already done the most critical work: we had surfaced the **real barriers** to accountability. And we started, not with training, but with **development**. As a learning community, we **Set the Space** and, while **Prompting with Purpose**, we were well on our way to SPARK IT!

The Illusion of Training as Transformation

There is a comforting clarity in training. It has steps. Templates. Learning objectives. It's repeatable, scalable, and measurable. And for many technical or procedural tasks, it's precisely what's needed. How to operate a tool. How to follow a protocol. How to comply with a policy.

But somewhere along the way, we began to use training as a default response to every performance gap, cultural tension, or leadership challenge. Does someone struggle to lead a team? Send them to a two-day leadership training. Morale is low? Let's launch a resilience course. Communication breakdowns? Time for a module.

We train because it's tidy. But human complexity is not tidy.

And that's where **facilitation comes in**—not to deliver knowledge, but to make space for awareness, growth, and insight.

The Difference Between Transfer and Transformation

Here's the essential distinction:

- **Training transfers knowledge.**
- **Development facilitates transformation.**

In training, the question is:

"What do they need to know?"

In development, the question becomes:

"Who are they becoming?"

Training says: "Here's the answer."
Development says: "Let's examine the question."
Training emphasizes competence.
Development cultivates **capacity**.

Training delivers solutions. Development supports evolution.

An Example of the Divide

In one organization, I watched two departments undergo different interventions. Department A received a "difficult conversations" training—a three-hour session with scripted phrases, slides, and dos and don'ts. Department B, instead, entered a facilitation process that included reflective questions, small-group stories, and role-play exercises rooted in their actual dynamics.

Six months later, Department A had neat workbooks and unchanged behavior. Department B had built a new norm: people were talking differently. They weren't just using new language—they had developed new courage.

That's what facilitation enables. Not a better technique, but deeper readiness.

Why This Distinction Matters More Than Ever

We're no longer living in an era where information is scarce. People are drowning in it. What's scarce is **sense-making**. And that's what development provides.

In a world of rapid change, high turnover, profound fatigue, and evolving expectations of leadership, people don't need more rules. They need space to reflect, reorient, and recommit to their leadership and work approach. They need a chance to **experiment with identity**, not just behavior. Who am I? Why do I do what I do? How do I define success?

And that only happens when we stop "delivering content" alone and start **facilitating consciousness**.

From Performance to Practice

To facilitate this shift means letting go of performance. You're not there to impress the group. You're there to provoke insight, to model presence, to hold tension with grace.

When someone says, "That really made me think," or "I saw something I hadn't before," you've done your job—even if they never remember your slide deck.

When they walk away not just with information, but with a different relationship to themselves, their work, or their people, that's development. That's your real impact.

You have brought the **SPARK IT!** framework to life!

Your Turn

Reflection: Are You Delivering or Developing?

Ask yourself before a session:

- Am I more focused on what I'll say—or what they'll discover?
- Where have I made space for surprise, story, or struggle?
- What does this group *need to wrestle with*—not just learn?
- What would it mean to succeed without being the center of attention?

Development requires us to trust the group's process as much as our own.

Closing: Don't Just Teach—Transform

You can train someone to follow a procedure. But you can't train someone to be brave. That's the work of development. And facilitation is how we make that work possible.

So the next time someone asks you to "train their people," pause. Ask what they want. Ask what they need.

And if what they need is transformation, then what they're asking for isn't training.

It's you.

My Reflections

Chapter 3 in a Nutshell:
In Life & At Work

In Life:

Learning isn't confined to classrooms,
it unfolds in moments of reflection, challenge, and growth. When we begin to see life experiences as developmental opportunities, we shift from passively receiving information to actively shaping who we become. Whether you're navigating a transition, rethinking your values, or helping a friend through change, ask: *"What am I learning about myself right now?"* Development is less about acquiring facts and more about expanding your way of seeing and being.

At Work:

Facilitators and leaders often default to training when what is needed is development. Training answers *how*, but development explores *why*, *when*, and *who you are* in action. Instead of overloading people with information, create a reflective space. Frame challenges as growth moments. Invite personal insights and self-assessment. Move from transactional learning toward transformational learning by designing experiences that change how people think, not just what they know.

ROBERT RADI

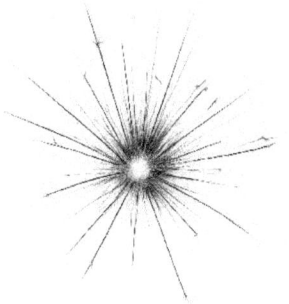

Chapter 4
Crafting Your Facilitation Philosophy

Facilitation isn't something you simply do. At some point—quietly, perhaps even unknowingly—it becomes who you are.

You start noticing the pause in a conversation that no one fills, and you make space for it. You begin asking questions that help people think more clearly, not just more quickly. You walk into a room wondering not "What will I say?" but "What will they need to discover?"

That shift doesn't happen because of a technique. It happens because you've begun to lead from a core—an internal orientation that shapes how you see others, how you show up, and how you hold space. That core is what I refer to as your **facilitation philosophy**.

What Is a Facilitation Philosophy?

A facilitation philosophy is not a mission statement. It's not a slogan or a set of principles printed on a poster. It's not something you can print on your favorite polo shirt. It's more intimate than that. It's your internal compass—something felt, lived, and refined over time.

It answers questions like:

- What do I believe about how people learn and grow?
- What kind of space do I strive to create?
- What role do I play when I facilitate—and what roles do I resist?
- How do I define success when I leave the room?

Your philosophy becomes the subtext of every session you lead. Whether you speak it aloud or not, it's there—in the choices you make, the energy you carry, the silence you hold, and the trust you extend.

Why It Matters

In environments where there is noise, speed, and pressure to perform, facilitation can easily become performative. We rush to impress. We hide behind frameworks. We lean on content when what's needed is **Kindling Connections**.

Your philosophy anchors you to something more profound than performance—it brings you back to presence.

It also helps you navigate the inevitable complexity: what to say, when to pivot, how to handle resistance, and when to hold silence. In those moments, you don't need a script. You need a center to **Iterate in Real Time**. And that center is built from your values, your beliefs, and your intention.

A Personal Story: When I Forgot My Philosophy

There was a session I led years ago that, by all external measures, was successful. The client was happy. The feedback was positive. The participants were engaged. But something in me felt off. What did I accomplish?

I had pushed through the agenda at full speed. I'd delivered with clarity, kept things on track, and moved the group through the flow. But I didn't listen deeply. I hadn't invited sufficient reflection. I hadn't made room for people to hear themselves think.

I had delivered the event, but I hadn't **facilitated their growth**.

Later that night, I asked myself, "What was I leading from?" The answer wasn't curiosity—it was pressure. I had temporarily abandoned my facilitation philosophy. And that experience reminded me why I needed one.

Because we all drift, a philosophy helps us find our way back.

Three Dimensions of Your Philosophy

Your facilitation philosophy emerges through three intertwined dimensions: your **values**, your **beliefs**, and your **intentions**.

1. Values: What Do You Stand for in the Room?

Your values are evident in how you relate to the group, not just in words, but in actions. If you value humility, you might defer to the group's wisdom before offering your own. If you value equity, you'll pay attention to who's being heard and who isn't.

Ask yourself:

- What are three values I want participants to experience when I facilitate?
- How do I express those values—not just say them?

Some examples:

- Respect
- Transparency
- Humor
- Generosity
- Accountability
- Patience
- Discovery

These aren't theoretical. They're what participants will experience—if they're real. And by real, I mean that you don't just espouse your values; you enact them consistently, congruently, and under all circumstances.

2. Beliefs: What Do You Believe About People and Learning?

Every facilitator holds implicit beliefs about learning, power, and change. Bringing them to light helps you lead with clarity.

Ask yourself:

- How do I believe people learn best?
- What do I believe about people's capacity to change?
- What's my role in helping someone make meaning?
- How about helping someone get unstuck?

You might believe:

- People don't resist change—they resist disconnection.
- Growth begins when people feel valued.
- Insight must be earned, not delivered.
- No one owns the whole truth alone.
- People are more likely to act on what they discover than what they're told.

Naming these beliefs helps you check for alignment. Are your methods honoring your convictions?

3. Intentions: Why Do You Facilitate?

Intentions are about purpose, not the group's outcomes, but yours. What drew you to facilitation in the first place?

Ask yourself:

- What do I hope to catalyze through facilitation?
- What do I want people to carry with them after they leave the room?
- What do I want to feel while I'm facilitating?

Maybe you facilitate the awakening of insight. To help people hear each other. To surface what's hidden. To break old patterns. To leave a room just a little more human than you found it.

That's not indulgent. That's your grounding force.

Drafting Your Philosophy

Now that you've explored values, beliefs, and intentions, you're ready to draft your personal facilitation philosophy. This is not a perfect statement. It's the **first version of a living compass**, something you can revise as your voice matures. There is no right or wrong way to do it. The only way to fail in developing a facilitating philosophy is not to do it at all.

Here's a simple structure to try:

"I facilitate to [intention] because I believe [core belief]. I aim to create spaces where [values are expressed], and I define success not by [external result], but by [internal alignment or participant experience]."

For example:

"I facilitate to help people reconnect with their wisdom because I believe clarity is often blocked, not missing. I aim to create spaces where curiosity, compassion, and ownership are present, and I define success not by how much content was covered, but by how much agency was awakened."

Yours may look very different. It should. That's the point.

Revisiting and Evolving

Your philosophy is not static. It will grow as you do. As you gain confidence, expand your range, and stretch your presence, you may find your intentions evolving. Your beliefs are refining. Your values are sharpening.

That's a sign you're facilitating, not from a script, but from yourself. So, revisit it. Rewrite it. And every so often, when a session leaves you off balance, go back to it and ask, "Was I leading from this—or away from it?"

From Reflection to Embodiment

There's a moment, often unnoticed, when your facilitation philosophy moves from something you *think about* to something you *live from*. It becomes embodied—not through repetition, but through reflection and realignment over time.

When embodied, your philosophy shows up even when you're off script. It's there when someone challenges you and you respond with grounded openness. It's in your timing—when to intervene and when to wait. It's in how you listen when no one is speaking.

This embodiment doesn't mean perfection; it means congruence. Your presence and your practice begin to match. And that congruence is what participants pick up on. Not the polish of your delivery, but the integrity behind it.

It also means that you become a tuning fork for the group. How grounded you are can regulate tension. Your curiosity can model risk-taking. Your presence can elevate the whole room. That's the quiet power of a lived philosophy—it leads without dominance.

Closing Thought: The Facilitator Behind the Method

Every model, question, framework, and tactic you use is only as powerful as the presence behind it. And that presence is formed by your philosophy.

Before people trust your process, they feel your posture.

Before they absorb your message, they notice your mindset.

Take the time to clarify who you're becoming as a facilitator. That's not vanity, it's integrity.

When your method aligns with your meaning, your facilitation becomes more than adequate. It becomes honest and memorable.

My Facilitating Philosophy

Chapter 4 in a Nutshell:
In Life & At Work

In Life:

Learning isn't confined to classrooms; it unfolds in moments of reflection, challenge, and growth. When we begin to see life experiences as developmental opportunities, we shift from passively receiving information to actively shaping who we become. Whether you're navigating a transition, rethinking your values, or helping a friend through change, ask: *"What am I learning about myself right now?"* Development is less about acquiring facts and more about expanding your perspective and being.

At Work:

Facilitators and leaders often default to training when what is needed is development. Training answers *how*, but development explores *why*, *when*, and *who you are* in action. Instead of overloading people with information, create a reflective space. Frame challenges as growth moments. Invite personal insights and self-assessment. Move from transactional learning toward transformational learning by designing experiences that change how people think, not just what they know.

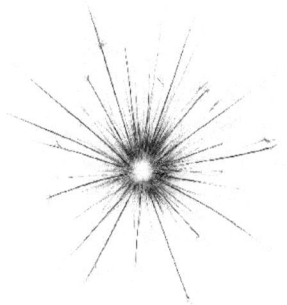

Chapter 5
Stories That Spark: Facilitating Meaning Through Narrative

It started as a research question during my doctoral studies.

I wasn't looking for a story—I was studying it. Specifically, I was exploring narrative as a qualitative research method to understand how people construct meaning in adverse conditions and how they communicate it. I wanted to know: *How do people communicate when faced with adversities, and how do they make sense of themselves?*

What I found wasn't just data. I discovered fragments of resilience, echoes of hope, and quiet reframing of identity. People weren't simply recounting events; they were reclaiming agency by

reconnecting to their values and principles.
Even in chaos, they shaped their stories with a thread of meaning. And that thread often became their way forward.

That realization changed how I saw facilitation. It wasn't just about guiding the process or asking good questions; it was about fostering a collaborative environment. It was about recognizing that people are constantly engaged in a silent form of storytelling. About their work. Their worth. Their possibilities. And when we facilitate well, we don't just move an agenda—we help them re-author their narratives.

American neuroscientist David Eagleman highlights that storytelling has developed effective structures over time, which captivate audiences by creating a sense of something significant happening, a problem to solve, or an unresolved tension. This engages the listener or reader, making them feel invested in the narrative and its outcome. In a nutshell, our brain loves stories.

A few years ago, I was facilitating a session for a group of federal managers. I introduced a model on adaptive communications, something I had used dozens of times. The framework was solid, the slides were sharp, and yet the room remained distant. Heads nodded, but there was no spark.

Then, without planning to, I put the slides aside and told a story.

It was about a supervisor I once coached who, despite her best intentions, was slowly disengaging her team by micromanaging every detail. She believed she was providing clarity, but what she was doing was removing autonomy. Through coaching, she realized this and shifted her approach. The transformation was tangible: the team regained energy, ownership, and momentum.

The moment I finished the story, a participant raised her hand and said, "That's me. I've been doing exactly that."

The room changed. We had entered a space of vulnerability, recognition, and learning.

Why the Brain Loves a Good Story

That shift wasn't magic—it was biology.

Modern neuroscience confirms what human history has always suggested: stories activate the brain in ways that raw data does not. When we hear facts, only the language centers of our brain are engaged. However, when we hear a story, multiple areas of the brain light up: the language, sensory, motor, and emotional regions. It's as if we are living the experience ourselves.

Research from neuroscientist Paul Zak has shown that emotionally engaging stories trigger the release of oxytocin, a hormone associated with empathy and trust. This is why stories build connections. They help us feel it before we think. And once we feel, we are more likely to remember, relate, and reflect. **That is part of Kindle Connections.**

In facilitation, that emotional resonance is what creates stickiness. Concepts become memorable not when they are explained, but when they are experienced through narrative.

From Fireside to Flipcharts: A Historical Thread

Long before books, slides, or whiteboards, human beings gathered around fires to share stories. It was through stories that knowledge was passed, warnings encoded, values reinforced, and identity preserved.

Stories were survival tools. They helped our ancestors navigate danger, build community, and transmit culture across generations. From learning about which animals posed a threat to social structure and relationships, stories were used to SPARK IT! way before I coined the acronym.

As philosopher Alasdair MacIntyre observed:

"Man is essentially a storytelling animal."

Even in modern times, we are constantly narrating—shaping experiences into plotlines. We don't just remember what happened; we also remember how it happened. We remember how it made us feel and what it meant to us.

This is why storytelling in facilitation is not a soft skill; it is a foundational skill. It allows us to honor a deeply human way of learning that predates formal education by thousands of years.

The Story as Meaning-Maker

Facilitation is the art of helping people make meaning together. And stories are tools of meaning-making. They help us navigate our way through complexity. They make the invisible visible. They move abstract ideas into embodied understanding.
When we share a story—whether it's a moment of failure, insight, confusion, or connection—we're not just sharing content. We're offering perspective, modeling vulnerability, and inviting co-creation.

Consider this example: I once opened a session on emotional intelligence not with a definition, but with a personal story of misreading a group dynamic—and the embarrassment that followed. That story led participants to recall moments of their own. Within minutes, the group had built a collective understanding of emotional intelligence without a single textbook citation.

That's facilitation through story—not top-down, but from the inside out.

The Architecture of an Effective Facilitation Story

Great facilitation stories are not long, polished monologues. They are compact, intentional, and emotionally anchored. They follow a natural rhythm:

Set the scene - Where are we? What's happening?

Introduce the tension - What problem or misalignment arose?

Describe the turning point - What realization or change occurred?

Reveal the insight - What was learned or gained?

Relate it back - Why does this matter to us right now?

Here's a simple illustration:

"I once worked with a senior leader who was puzzled by his team's silence. 'I always ask for input,' he said. However, when I observed him in action, his questions were rhetorical, and his tone was final. I shared this with him. He was stunned. He genuinely thought he was inviting collaboration. That moment changed how he framed every future conversation."

Short. Real. Reflective.

And it mirrors the kind of shifts we hope participants will experience themselves.

Facilitators as Story Stewards, Not Storytellers

You don't have to be a great performer. You don't need a perfect script. What you need is purpose. The story should serve the group's learning, not your ego.
This means being willing to share your missteps. To name ambiguity. To offer experiences that provoke—not conclude—thinking.

And, crucially, it means creating space for others to share.

Instead of asking, "What do you think of this concept?" try:

"Can you think of a time this played out at work?"

"What's a story that illustrates this challenge in action?"

"Has anyone here experienced something like this?"

When participants share stories, the room becomes a co-learning ecosystem. Power shifts from the facilitator to the group. Meaning expands.

On Self-Deprecating Humor

One of the most disarming forms of storytelling is self-deprecating humor. It lowers defenses, builds connections, and signals that we take the work seriously, but we don't take *ourselves* too seriously.

When a facilitator shares a brief, honest moment of failure or awkwardness, it invites the group to exhale. It says: *"This is a space where imperfection is allowed."* In a world that often rewards polish and performance, self-deprecating humor reminds people that learning, growth, and even leadership are fundamentally human endeavors. Used sparingly and sincerely, it transforms the facilitator from a distant expert into a relatable guide. Someone who is not above the struggle but is inside it with others.

Some of the most beloved public figures have leveraged this kind of humor to establish rapport. Abraham Lincoln famously defused tension during a debate by saying, "If I were two-faced, would I be wearing this one?" President Barack Obama often poked fun at his ears or his graying hair to ease the audience into more complex conversations. Comedian Tina Fey has built an entire body of work around owning her awkwardness and flaws in a way that makes others feel seen. These aren't punchlines, they're trust signals. They make the room more human. And in facilitation, humanity is a superpower.

Narrative in Everyday Facilitation

Narrative isn't reserved for grand speeches or brand campaigns; it's how we make sense of the world in conversation, conflict, change, and growth. As facilitators, whether in a boardroom or around the breakfast table, we are constantly working with stories—those we inherit, those we challenge, and those we help shape.

At work, you may notice a colleague stuck in a loop: "Leadership doesn't listen, so there's no point in speaking up." That's not just a complaint, it's a story. One that protects, deflects, and limits. Effective facilitation doesn't confront that story head-on. It gently rewrites it by offering new experiences of being heard, valued, and respected.

At home, a teenager muttering, "Nothing I do matters," may not respond to a pep talk. But if you ask, "When did you start feeling that way?"–you will open the door to a different kind of story. One where emotion has space, and connection can grow.

Even in casual settings—such as family dinners, PTA meetings, and group chats among friends—narratives are alive. They shape how people present themselves, how they speak (or remain silent), how they trust, and how they resist. When we facilitate these everyday exchanges with presence and care, we begin to loosen the grip of rigid stories and make space for more generative ones.

This is where narrative becomes a facilitative act, not something we tell, but something we help unfold. And in doing so, we don't just guide a group forward. We help individuals re-author their self-perception and envision what's possible next.

Philosophy Meets Practice: The Narrative Self

Whether you're leading a team meeting, mentoring a colleague, or guiding a conversation around your kitchen table, one truth holds steady: people make sense of their experiences through stories. We don't just think—we narrate.

Philosopher Paul Ricoeur called this *narrative identity*: the idea that we come to understand ourselves through the stories we live, tell, and revise. Our past choices, our current challenges, our future hopes—they're all organized into arcs of meaning.

Facilitators—professional or informal—tap into this every day. We don't push people toward answers. We create space for insight. We help others author meaning by reflecting on where they've been, where they are, and where they might go.

Whether in a corporate workshop or a one-on-one conversation, this approach matters. It's how people discover agency—not through instruction, but through self-authored insight.

When facilitation honors narrative identity, transformation isn't forced. It unfolds.

Closing: Story as an Act of Connection

In every meaningful exchange, there comes a moment when logic alone won't carry the weight. That's when story steps in—not as entertainment, but as a bridge.

A bridge between what's being said and what's truly felt.
A bridge between the facilitator and the group.
A bridge between where someone is and where they're ready to go next.

Story roots concepts in lived experience. It translates abstract models into relatable meaning. It turns "what" into "why it matters."

So whether you're guiding a workshop, helping your child wrestle with a tough day, or diffusing tension on a community board, don't underestimate the power of a well-chosen story. Not to persuade—to connect. Not to impress—to reveal.

Because what people remember isn't the clever quote or polished framework.
They remember the moment they felt seen.
They remember when your story helped them hear their own story more clearly.

And that's what lingers long after the meeting ends or the dinner plates are cleared.

That's the spark that stays lit.

Your Turn

Facilitation Exercises

Exercise 1: Five-Minute Story Jam

- **Objective**: Practice concise, emotionally resonant storytelling.
- **Instructions**:
  - Give participants a common prompt (e.g., *"A time I learned from failure"* or *"A moment I changed my mind"*).
  - Give 3 minutes to jot down the scene, tension, turning point, and takeaway.
  - In pairs, each person tells their story in under 2 minutes.
  - After each round, the listener offers one word in answer to this question: *What stayed with you?*

Debrief: Discuss how storytelling created connection, insight, or new understanding—even with strangers.

Exercise 2: Story Autopsy

- **Objective**: Analyze stories for impact and structure.
- **Instructions**:
  - Share a recorded clip (TED talk, podcast, training video) where a story is used.

➢ As a group, identify:
- What made it engaging?
- What emotion did it evoke?
- What was the narrative arc?
- How did it support learning?

Debrief: Transition to, "How can we build our own stories with the same clarity and impact?"

Exercise 3: Prompt-and-Reflect Circles

- **Objective**: Elicit real experiences from the room to co-create learning.
- **Instructions**: Use prompts that invite story-based reflection:
    - ➢ *"Tell us about a time you misunderstood someone at work."*
    - ➢ *"Share a story about a team breakthrough you experienced."*
    - ➢ *"When did you feel most heard—or unheard—in a group?"*

The facilitator sets respectful norms. Participants reflect briefly in writing and then share their thoughts in triads or as a whole group.

Debrief: Highlight the diversity of insights that emerged from shared experiences, rather than abstract theorizing.

Reflection Prompt

Think back to a time when a story changed how you saw a person, problem, or possibility. What made the story stick? Was it the emotion, the relatability, the vulnerability, or something else?

Now ask yourself:

- What stories live in your own leadership or facilitation journey?
- Which one might offer insight to others, not because you succeeded, but because you learned?

Please write a short version (no more than 150 words) and give it a working title.

Story Skeleton Template

Use this fill-in-the-blanks format to build your facilitation stories with clarity and resonance:

1. **Scene**:
   "I was facilitating a session for [audience/context]..."

2. **Tension**:
   "What I noticed was [disconnect/challenge/surprise]..."

3. **Turning Point**:
   "The shift happened when [person/group realization/action]..."

4. **Insight**:
   "That experience taught me that [key insight]..."

5. **Bridge to Others**:
   "And I share this today because [why it matters to this group/context]..."

My Narrative Approach

Chapter 5 in a Nutshell:
In Life & At Work

In Life:

Stories help us make sense of chaos, hold on to meaning, and navigate adversity. In moments of uncertainty or hardship, crafting and revisiting your personal narrative can be a grounding experience. Ask yourself: *What story am I telling myself about this experience? Is it empowering or limiting?* When you reframe your story—not to deny reality, but to deepen perspective—you can reclaim agency and compassion. Stories connect us not only to others but to our evolving selves.

At Work:

Storytelling isn't just a performance skill; it's a facilitation superpower. Stories engage attention, reveal values, and move teams beyond data into meaning. As a facilitator, you can use narrative to anchor abstract ideas, humanize complex topics, or model vulnerability. Encourage others to share stories—not just polished ones, but real ones. Story-based prompts, metaphor exercises, or journey maps can unlock powerful insights in teams. Great facilitation sparks shared stories that outlast the session.

ROBERT RADI

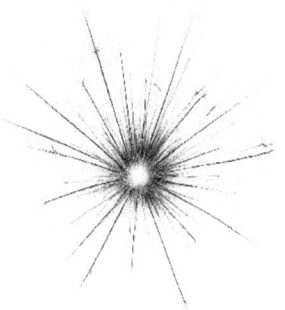

Chapter 6

The Courage to Adjust: Responsive Facilitation

A participant once told me, after a session, "You really listened. Not just to what we said, but to what we didn't." It stayed with me, not as praise, but as a reminder: facilitation is not performance. It is being present. It is about listening objectively and intuitively, rather than subjectively. It is about managing our attention.

Responsive facilitation is the practice of being *fully present in the room*. It's the ability to read energy, absorb feedback—verbal and nonverbal—and adjust without apology or defensiveness. It takes more than experience. It takes courage.

To respond honestly, you must release control.

The Myth of the Perfect Agenda

Facilitators, especially new ones, often cling to their agenda like a life raft. And understandably so. We spend hours crafting flow, timing activities, and designing transitions. The structure provides safety for us and the group.

But here's the truth: **real learning is not linear**. People don't experience insight on a clock. They arrive at understanding through confusion, detours, questions, discomfort, and unexpected resonance. And if we're too tightly tethered to our plan, we'll miss the moment when the room is ready for something more profound.

The best facilitators don't throw out structure; they hold it **lightly**. They sense when a group needs to dwell in a moment longer or skip what no longer serves. They understand the difference between content coverage and meaningful engagement.

As facilitator Meg Wheatley put it:

"We can't be creative if we refuse to be confused."

Responsive Facilitation in Everyday Life

Responsive facilitation isn't just for workshops or team offsites. It's for hallway conversations, dinner table check-ins, and tough talks with your teenager. Any time people gather, there's a flow beneath the surface—and a chance to meet that flow with intention rather than control.

At work, it might mean pausing the agenda to acknowledge tension that's quietlyderailing progress. At home, it might mean sensing when a loved one needs space before they can speak. In community spaces, it's recognizing when a group is hungry for validation more than instruction.

In all of these moments, responsiveness begins with attention. It asks us to tune in, not just to what's being said, but to what's being felt, what's shifting, and what's emerging. It requires slowing down just enough to notice.

We often equate leadership with direction. But facilitative leadership lives in the pause, the pivot, the "let's hold here for a moment." It doesn't mean giving up structure. It means listening deeply enough to know when to flex it in service of something real.

Reflection-in-Action: Learning as You Lead

The late philosopher and organizational theorist Donald Schön coined the term *reflection-in-action*—the ability to think about what you're doing while you're doing it. It's a hallmark of expert practice across fields: surgeons adjusting mid-procedure, jazz musicians improvising mid-song, educators shifting mid-lesson.

In facilitation, reflection-in-action means tuning in not only to what is happening, but also to *how* it's happening. It means asking yourself in real time:

- Is the group with me, or are they resisting?
- Did that land as I intended, or did it create confusion?
- Is the room ready to move on, or is something still unresolved?

It's not about second-guessing—it's about being in *dynamic dialogue* with the experience you're facilitating.

Managing Our Attention: The Three Levels of Listening

Facilitation lives or dies in the quality of your listening. Not just hearing, but *listening*—deeply, responsively, without rehearsing your reply while someone else is still speaking.

Most people think they're good listeners. However, what they often do is simply wait for their turn. Effective facilitation—and meaningful human connection—requires moving beyond that. It requires understanding the *levels* of listening.

Let's break them down:

Level 1: Subjective Listening - "How does this relate to me?"

This is the most common and automatic level. At Level 1, we listen through the filter of our own experience, needs, and emotions. We're not really tracking the other person; we're noticing how their words impact *us*.

You might catch yourself thinking:
- "That happened to me once..."
- "I wouldn't do it that way..."
- "I need to make sure they understand my point next."

Subjective listening isn't wrong; it's human. But it's also limiting. It centers *your narrative* instead of theirs. And when you're facilitating, it can make people feel unseen or subtly dismissed.

Level 2: Objective Listening - "What are they actually saying?"

Here, your attention shifts *to* the other person. You're no longer scanning for personal relevance—you're entirely focused on content, clarity, and meaning. You listen for them.

You notice:
- Word choice
- Tone
- Pace
- Gaps between what's said and what's left unsaid

At this level, your curiosity is active. You reflect. You paraphrase. You ask open-ended questions to help them go deeper.
Objective listening builds trust. It makes people feel heard—not corrected or redirected, but *understood*.

Level 3: Intuitive Listening - "What's really going on here?"

At Level 3, you listen with more than your ears. You tune into what's underneath the words—energy, emotion, hesitation, incongruence, and environment.

You sense:
- The tension in someone's body language
- The fear behind their deflection
- The unspoken longing behind their complaint

This is the kind of listening that makes people say, "You really got me." It's quiet, attuned, and expansive. It's where facilitation becomes art.
Intuitive listening takes practice, presence, and humility. But when you operate at this level, something powerful happens: people hear *themselves* more clearly.

Bringing It All Together

All three levels have a place. Sometimes you need to start with the Subjective level to notice your own reactions. Then shift into the Objective level to ground the exchange. And when the moment calls for it, step into the Intuitive level to uncover what's truly at stake.
Facilitators who move fluidly across these levels—at work, at home, or in the world—help others feel *heard and move toward clarity*.
And that's when the real work begins.

The Emotional Labor of Adjusting

Responsive facilitation requires not just intellectual flexibility but *emotional resilience*. To adjust your course publicly—especially in front of skeptical or senior participants—can feel vulnerable. We worry:

- Will I seem unprepared?
- Will I lose credibility?
- Will this derail the session?

But often, the opposite is true.

When you respond authentically to what the room needs, you gain trust. You model humility. You show that this is not about your ego—it's about their growth. And that unlocks permission for others to show up more fully as well.

One of the most powerful moments I've witnessed in a session came when a facilitator noticed tension rising and paused mid-activity. He stepped back and said, "I sense this isn't working the way I'd hoped. Can we take a moment and name what's happening?"

What followed was ten minutes of honest, constructive conversation. The group not only reengaged—they respected the facilitator more for noticing, naming, and adjusting.

That's the quiet bravery of responsive facilitation.

The Compass Over the Map

Think of your session plan not as a map, but as a compass. The destination may be fixed—supporting growth and deepening understanding—but the route will change based on the terrain.

What does that look like in practice?

- **When energy drops**, pause. Ask what's present. Shift formats.

- **When someone raises a disruptive but important question**, lean in. Let the group explore.

- **When an activity falls flat**, don't push through—debrief it with curiosity: "That didn't go where I thought it might. Why do you think that is?"

- **When the timing runs out**, don't panic. Prioritize depth over breadth. Trust that what *did* happen was enough.

This is not about abandoning goals. It's about honoring emergence. It's about being *responsibly improvisational*.

Examples in Motion

Let's say you're leading a session on psychological safety, and a participant unexpectedly shares a painful experience of being publicly shamed by a past leader. The room goes quiet. What do you do?

You could return to your planned slide on "the five elements of safety"—or you could pause, acknowledge the vulnerability, and invite others to reflect.

The latter choice may delay your timeline. But it deepens the moment. It tells the group: *We are not just here to cover material. We are here to matter to each other.*

Or imagine you're midway through a breakout group activity and the groups clearly aren't connecting. Rather than forcing completion, you pause and say:

"Let's come back together early. I'm noticing some friction or confusion—can we talk about what's emerging?"

This adjustment not only rescues the session—it turns the moment into a learning opportunity.

Responsive ≠ Reactive

To be clear, responsiveness is not the same as reactivity.

- *Reactive facilitation* is driven by fear, approval-seeking, or discomfort. It looks like over-correcting, apologizing, or abandoning the agenda at the first sign of resistance.
- *Responsive facilitation* is grounded, intentional, and principled. It's about noticing, pausing, and choosing deliberately how to move forward.

The difference lies in *awareness*. And the confidence to stay rooted even as you shift.

Closing: Progress Over Perfection

You will have sessions where the energy is off, where an activity misfires, where the group is hard to read. And you'll be tempted to blame yourself. Don't.

Remember: **facilitation is not about control—it's about stewardship**. You're not here to manufacture a flawless experience. You're here to tend the learning environment with care, awareness, and courage.

The more willing you are to adjust, the more real the session becomes. And often, the most potent moments aren't the ones you planned. They're the ones you *noticed*.

Responsive facilitation isn't flashy. But it's where the real magic lives.

Your Turn

Reflection Prompt

Think back to a time when you followed the plan even though your gut told you not to. What was the cost? What might have changed if you had paused and responded instead?

Now flip the lens:

Recall a moment when you broke from the script—what gave you the courage to adjust, and what did it unlock for the group?

Write for 5-7 minutes. Then share in pairs or reflect silently on the patterns that emerge.

Practice Exercises

Exercise 1: Signal Scanning

Objective: Train attention to group cues in real time.

- During any group session (even as a participant), practice noticing:
    - Verbal signals (repetition, confusion, silence)
    - Non-verbal cues (fidgeting, eye contact, leaning out)
    - Energy shifts (momentum, resistance, openness)

Debrief: What did you notice that others may have missed? What would you have adjusted if you had been facilitating?

Exercise 2: Scenario Jam – "Adjust or Anchor?"

Objective: Strengthen decision-making under pressure.

- Present 3-5 facilitation scenarios (see sample below).
- For each, ask:
    - Would you *adjust* or *anchor*?
    - What would guide your decision?
    - What values or outcomes are at stake?

Sample Scenario:
You're leading a discussion on collaboration. A senior participant interrupts and shifts focus to leadership dysfunction in their department. The room turns tense but curious. Do you redirect or explore?

Debrief: Discuss the trade-offs between structure and emergence. Emphasize intentionality over avoidance.

Real-Time Adjustment Checklist: "The Facilitator's Gut-Check"

When something feels off, pause and ask yourself:

1. **What's really happening in the room right now?**
    - Is energy rising or dropping?
    - Are people confused, disengaged, or eager to go deeper?

2. **Is my plan still serving the group's needs?**
    - Am I more focused on covering content or advancing learning?

3. **What are my instincts telling me?**
    - Do I feel discomfort, fear, or intuition?
    - Is this a moment to lean in or step back?
4. **What are the risks of adjusting and of not adjusting?**
    - What will be lost or gained by changing direction?
5. **How can I invite the group in?**
    - Can I name the shift transparently? ("Here's what I'm noticing . . . What do you think we need?")
6. **How will I close the loop?**
    - If I shift course, how will I ensure we return to core outcomes?

Post this checklist near your agenda or notes—it's not just a troubleshooting tool. It's a reminder that **you're allowed to respond**, and that responsiveness is a core facilitation skill, not a sign of weakness.

Chapter 6 in a Nutshell:
In Life & At Work

In Life:

Life rarely follows a script—and neither should you. The ability to pivot, recalibrate, and adjust your tone or approach is not a weakness; it's wisdom in motion. When conversations go off course, or when someone's energy shifts, try pausing instead of pushing through. Ask yourself: "What's really needed right now?" That single moment of inquiry can prevent disconnection and deepen understanding. Whether you're parenting, partnering, or simply navigating an awkward moment, responsiveness allows relationships to breathe and realign.

At Work:

Meetings, teams, and group dynamics are living systems, not fixed agendas. A skilled facilitator (or manager, or team lead) learns to read the room—not just by listening to words, but by sensing energy, silence, resistance, and readiness. Adjusting in real time might mean simplifying an exercise, shortening a discussion, or amplifying unexpected insights. Don't cling to your plan—serve the moment. Responsive facilitation builds trust because it demonstrates that you're not just following a process; you're attuned to the people involved.

ROBERT RADI

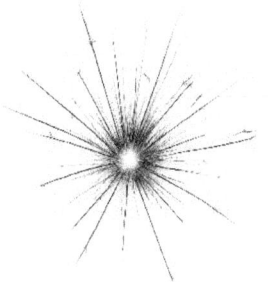

Chapter 7

Building the Emotional Infrastructure: Trust, Empathy, and Inclusive Dialogue

Before we ask people to think critically, take risks, or open up, we must ask: Do they feel safe enough to do so? This is a critical prompt in any setting, at home, at work, and with friends.

Before we invite dialogue, we must ensure that we've created the conditions for it to matter and be effective.

This is the work of emotional infrastructure —the often-invisible foundation that determines whether a session merely delivers content or fosters genuine transformation. Content may inform, but emotional infrastructure determines whether it's absorbed, whether it sticks, and whether it moves someone to act.

Everyday Emotional Infrastructure

You don't need a facilitation title to build trust. You don't need flipcharts or slide decks to create inclusion. Emotional infrastructure isn't confined to training sessions—it's formed in the flow of everyday conversations: a moment of listening in a team huddle, a pause during a family disagreement, or a coffee chat that opens something deeper.
Emotional infrastructure is the *felt safety* that allows people to speak honestly, disagree respectfully, and connect meaningfully. In the SPARK IT! framework, this foundation is woven through multiple elements, especially:

- **Set the Space**, which establishes clarity, trust, and a sense of purpose.
- **Kindle Connection**, which builds empathy and shared meaning.
- **Respond with Curiosity**, which replaces reflex with attuned inquiry.
- And **Iterate in Real Time**, which demonstrates respect for what's emergent, not just what's planned.

These moves aren't theoretical. They show up in the smallest interactions:

- **At work**, it's saying, "Before we jump in—how's everyone landing in the room today?"

- **At home**, it's asking, "What do you need from me right now—support, space, or just someone to listen?"

- **With friends**, it's offering curiosity over correction: "Tell me more about what that felt like."

These are the moments that build emotional infrastructure—slowly, authentically, and consistently. They communicate, "You matter here. Your voice belongs. You are heard."
Without this foundation, even the most well-crafted prompts or learning strategies fall flat. But with it, the room becomes braver, the silence becomes fertile, and dialogue becomes transformative.

So, whether you're facilitating a session or simply navigating your daily life, return to this question:

Am I creating conditions that foster trust, empathy, and inclusion?

If yes, then you're already facilitating—everywhere you go.

Micro-Moves That Build Trust in the Moment

Facilitating emotional infrastructure isn't about grand gestures; it's about making consistent, micro-level adjustments. Here are a few you can integrate into everyday settings:

- **Name the moment**: "Let's pause—I sense there's something unspoken here."

- **Invite, don't demand**: "You're welcome to share, but only if it feels right."

- **Acknowledge tension without solving it**: "It's okay for us to sit with this discomfort."

- **Offer presence, not polish**: "I don't have the answer, but I'm here to explore it with you."

- **Reflect inclusion**: "I noticed we haven't heard from everyone yet. Is there a voice we're missing?"

Each small move signals safety, dignity, and respect. Over time, they become the invisible scaffolding that supports deeper dialogue and more profound connections.

You Are Now the Architect

Facilitation isn't just a cognitive exchange. It's an emotional transaction. And if we don't understand how trust, empathy, and inclusion work beneath the surface, we may misread resistance, mislabel silence, or mistake politeness for engagement.

Let's take a closer look at what holds a room together.

1. Psychological Safety: The Hidden Prerequisite

Harvard researcher Amy Edmondson defined psychological safety as "a belief that one will not be punished or humiliated for speaking up with ideas, questions, concerns, or mistakes."

That belief is not automatically present in every group. It has to be cultivated—and that's often the unseen labor of facilitation.

Ask yourself, do people in this room feel safe enough:

- to be wrong?
- to say "I don't know"?
- to challenge the dominant voice?

- to bring their whole self across lines of power, role, perspectives, and backgrounds?

If the answer is no–or even "maybe not"–your job is not just facilitating a topic. Your job is promoting the creation of trust. And trust begins with your tone, body language, and modeling. When facilitators reveal vulnerability, admit mistakes, and show curiosity instead of certainty, they signal that this space is about growth, not performance.

2. The Neuroscience of Emotion and Belonging

We are wired for connection.

Neuroscience tells us that when we feel excluded or unsafe, the brain triggers the same pain centers activated by physical harm. **The amygdala–the brain's threat detector–goes on alert**, and we shift into protection mode. Cognitive resources become narrow–creativity, empathy, and higher-order reasoning decline.

Conversely, when we feel seen and included, the **prefrontal cortex becomes activated, allowing us to reflect, engage, and process with greater** openness. This is not abstract science; it's visible in every room.
That awkward silence after someone shares something personal. The way a participant suddenly shuts down after a dismissive comment. These are not signs of disinterest. They are signs of emotional rupture.

Facilitators must learn to recognize them, repair them, and–better yet–design to prevent them.

3. Empathy Before Instruction

There's a facilitator habit that sounds helpful but often creates distance. It goes like this:

"I know exactly what you mean. That happened to me too . . . "
In the moment, we're trying to relate. But often, what people need isn't similarity—it's **validation**. Not "me too," but "tell me more."

Empathy in facilitation means slowing down before offering interpretation. It means listening for what's underneath a comment. It means reading the emotional field, not just the verbal content.

Ask yourself:
- Am I seeking to understand—or to move on?
- Am I holding space—or filling it?

Sometimes the most powerful facilitation tool is a pause that says: "You matter."

4. Inclusion as Design, Not Intention

Many facilitators consider themselves inclusive because they hold inclusive values. However, inclusion is not just a belief; it's a **practice**.

- Do you rotate who speaks first in discussions?
- Do you use varied modalities (writing, talking, visuals) to accommodate different processing styles?
- Do you explicitly invite quieter voices without forcing disclosure?
- Do your materials reflect diverse identities and perspectives?

True inclusion is not just about who's in the room; it's about *who the room is built for.*

And inclusion is not just about content—it's about **access to influence**.

Who gets to shape the direction of the discussion? Whose insights are picked up, echoed, or acted upon?

A truly inclusive session leaves participants not just informed but empowered to act on the outcomes of the session.

5. Facilitators as Emotional Anchors

Groups unconsciously calibrate their emotional tone to match that of the facilitator. If you're anxious, they contract. If you're grounded, they expand. If you rush, they check out.

This is not about suppressing emotion. It's about being *attuned* to yourself and others. You don't have to be flawless. You have to be honest, regulated, and spacious.

One of the most potent tools you carry isn't in your slide deck—it's in your breath. Your composure. Your willingness to stay present, even when emotions rise. When you hold steady, the group trusts they can bring more of themselves to the surface.

Emotional Infrastructure in Practice: Design Questions

Ask yourself as you prepare a session:
- How will participants know this space is safe to take risks?

- What signals will I send (verbal and non-verbal) to establish trust?

- How do I make room for discomfort without rushing to solve it?

- How do I ensure no one dominates, and everyone feels they belong?

- What will I do if exclusion happens in the room?

Your answers don't need to be perfect. They need to be practiced.

Reflection Prompt

When have you felt deeply included in a group? What created that feeling?
When have you felt unseen or unsafe in a group setting? What caused that breakdown—and what might have repaired it?
How can you utilize these experiences to inform your approach to facilitating spaces for others?

Let me share with you the following:
- Sample *group agreement* language
- A one-page *inclusion design* checklist
- A short *case vignette* showing repair of emotional rupture mid-session

Sample Group Agreements Language

These group agreements (sometimes called "working agreements" or "collaborative norms") can be co-created or offered at the start of a session to establish psychological safety and emotional integrity. You can present them as a starting point and invite additions or edits. In virtual environments, I found it beneficial to share some effective norms to get the ball rolling, then invite participants to expand on them.

Suggested Agreements for Inclusive Dialogue

- Speak from your own experience, not on behalf of others.
- Listen to understand, not to reply.
- Allow for discomfort—it's part of learning.
- Take space, make space: be aware of your participation.
- It's okay to pass. Silence is participation, too.
- Assume positive intent, but own your impact.
- What's shared here stays here; what's learned here leaves here.

Facilitator Tip: Pause to ask, *"What would make this space feel safer or supportive for you?"* The responses become the co-authored social contract.

One-Page Inclusion Design Checklist

Use this checklist during planning and facilitation to ensure emotional and cognitive inclusion:

1. Access & Participation
- Are materials accessible to different learning styles (visual, auditory, kinesthetic)?
- Have I provided alternatives to verbal participation (e.g., chat, notes, polls)?
- Does the tech setup (in-person or virtual) allow for equitable contributions?

2. Power & Voice
- Am I actively drawing out quieter voices and limiting "overcontributors"?
- Have I acknowledged potential identity-based dynamics (race, gender, role, etc.)?
- Am I modeling curiosity when participants push back or diverge?

3. Language & Framing
- Is my language inclusive, avoiding jargon, idioms, or assumptions?
- Have I considered how culture might affect how safety, risk, or disagreement is expressed?

4. Flexibility & Care
- Is there built-in space for emotional processing or breaks?
- Have I offered permission to "pass," opt out, or speak privately if needed?

Revisit mid-session. Adjust accordingly.

Mini Case Vignette: Repairing a Moment of Exclusion

Context: You're facilitating a collaboration session. A participant named Jordan shares a personal story about feeling dismissed in meetings. Another participant, Pat, interjects with, "I think people are just too sensitive these days."

The room stiffens. Jordan looks down. Silence.

What you could do as a facilitator:

You could consider one of these approaches, or a combination of them:

- **Pause and name**: "Let's hold for a moment. I noticed some tension. I want to make sure we're staying present with what was just shared."
- **Acknowledge impact without shaming**: "Jordan just offered something vulnerable and important. Pat, I know

your intention wasn't to shut that down, but the impact might have felt that way."

- **Recenter purpose**: "We're here to explore how different perspectives shape collaboration. That means staying curious, even when we disagree."

- **Invite reflection**: "Let's take a breath. Maybe turn to a partner and ask: 'What helps me stay open when I hear something that challenges me?'"

What happens next?
Often, the room exhales. People re-engage. Jordan feels protected without Pat feeling like she was singled out. You've modeled *repair*, which may be the most crucial emotional infrastructure skill of all.

Your Turn

Closing: Emotional Infrastructure Is Strategic Infrastructure

Trust isn't just a feeling; it's a precondition for thinking clearly, connecting authentically, and learning meaningfully. That's why emotional infrastructure isn't a "soft skill"—it's a strategic skill. Without it, facilitation becomes performative. With it, it becomes transformative.

The SPARK IT! framework is not just a sequence of techniques. It's a way of being that makes trust visible and emotional integrity actionable. Every time you **Set the Space**, **Kindle Connection**, or **Respond with Curiosity**, you are engineering the conditions where people can learn, grow, and contribute—without fear.

Reflection Prompts: Reconnecting to SPARK IT!

Set the Space
What unspoken signals—tone, posture, pacing—am I sending before a word is spoken? How can I adjust those signals to foster trust and openness from the start?
Respond with Curiosity
When I encounter resistance or discomfort, do I lean in with curiosity or try to move past it? What would it look like to stay present and ask "Tell me more" instead of "Let's move on"?
Kindle Connection
How am I actively cultivating connection in the room? Whose story, silence, or energy might be trying to speak—and how can I invite it into the conversation?

Chapter 7 in a Nutshell:
In Life & At Work

In Life:

At home and in your relationships, people aren't looking for perfection—they're looking for presence. Emotional infrastructure begins with empathy: the willingness to understand before being understood. When trust is present, people speak more honestly and listen more generously. You don't need advanced techniques; you need intentional curiosity. Ask more open questions. Practice pausing before responding. And remember, inclusion isn't about agreement—it's about respect. When people feel seen and safe, connection deepens.

At Work:

Workplaces run on more than processes—they run on emotional bandwidth. If your meetings feel performative or disengaged, it may be that trust hasn't been built or maintained. Facilitation is not just about directing conversation; it's about inviting courage. Use empathy as a leadership tool. Normalize vulnerability by being the first to acknowledge uncertainty or tension. Set psychological safety as a precondition, not a bonus. Inclusive dialogue is not a "nice to have"—it's the foundation for innovation, cohesion, and shared ownership.

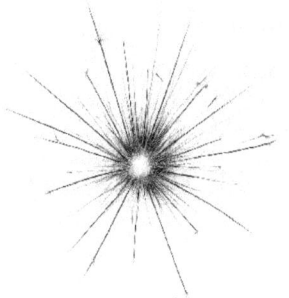

Chapter 8

Engagement Design: Tools, Prompts, and Tactics

Facilitators are not lecturers per se, although some "lecturettes" may be part of the process. Instead, they are designers of engagement. And every attempt at engagement is a deliberate interplay of **timing, tone, tools, and trust**.

Unfortunately, engagement is often misunderstood. It's not about high energy, fancy icebreakers, or getting people to "talk more." Recently, I facilitated a leadership course for a federal enforcement agency. Although the input provided by the participants was brief in terms of word count, it was impactful due to the level of attunement present in the room.

Authentic engagement happens when people feel valued, relevant, and invited to contribute meaningfully to something that matters.

The best facilitators don't just *keep people busy*; they **activate a sense of purpose**. They invite reflection, unlock connection, and spark shared discovery. And they do so not by accident, but through thoughtful design.

Design Engagement in Everyday Facilitation

You don't need a whiteboard or a workshop agenda to design engagement. Every conversation you initiate—whether at work, at home, or in your community—offers a chance to apply the same principles that drive effective facilitation.

Everyday facilitation is not about performance; it's about presence and intention. And engagement design in these contexts is about crafting moments that feel open, honest, and catalytic.

It could look like this:

- At work, rather than launching into a meeting agenda, you ask: "Before we dive in, is there anything top-of-mind that needs our attention first?" That single shift in tone transforms the room from one of compliance to one of collaboration.

- At home, instead of advising your teenager, you ask: "If you had a do-over for today, what would you keep the same and what would you change?" You've just created a space for self-reflection, not judgment.

- In a community setting, instead of calling on the loudest voice, you say: "Let's hear from someone we haven't heard yet—what's coming up for you?" That's engagement by design—not force.

The common thread? You're not trying to control the conversation—you're curating the conditions for others to feel safe enough to step in.

Think of these moments as micro-designs:

- A well-timed pause
- A reframed question
- A subtle shift in tone
- A decision to listen longer

Each of these is a tool, not in the mechanical sense, but in the human sense. They are tools that honor attention, build momentum, and foster meaningful participation.

Whether you're leading a team retreat or sitting around a dinner table, designing engagement means remembering that people engage most when they feel *seen, safe, and significant*.

And those are conditions you can create, moment by moment.

1. Understand the Architecture of Engagement

Facilitated sessions unfold in **arcs**. A great session flows like a good story:

- **Open the space** with clarity, tone, and purpose.
- **Activate curiosity** through inquiry and exploration.
- **Deepen insight** through structured reflection or interaction.
- **Surface application**, which helps participants synthesize and apply their learning.
- **Close with resonance**—emotionally and cognitively.

This arc doesn't have to be linear. It can loop, spiral, or shift. But it must have an intentional rhythm. Engagement suffers most when we **overplan content and underplan process**.

2. Choose the Right Tool for the Right Moment

Not all engagement tools are equal. And none of them work all the time. The key is **alignment**—selecting the right activity or prompt for the group, goal, and moment.

Here are categories of facilitation tools and when to use them:

Tool Type	Use When You Want to . . .	Sample Tactics
Check-Ins	Open up, build presence and safety	One word check-in, metaphor prompt.
Prompt-Based Reflection	Activate introspection or uncover assumptions	Journaling, guided questions, polarity mapping
Peer Dialogue	Build empathy, deepen understanding	Think-pair-share, triad stories, peer coaching
Synthesis Tools	Help participants make meaning or connect ideas	Affinity clustering, visual mapping, mind clouds
Group Movement	Shift energy, surface patterns, involve the whole room	Spectrum line, stand-up responses, gallery walks
Breakout Rooms	Encourage safe risk-taking, equalize voice	Scenario jams, case study analysis.
Creative Expression	Access emotion, metaphor, or nonlinear insights	Draw-your-leadership, haiku reflections, storytelling skeletons

Remember: the *tool is only as powerful as the intention behind it.*

3. Design for Introverts, Skeptics, and Risk-Takers Alike

Engagement is not one-size-fits-all. Some people need space to think before they speak. Others prefer private processing. Still others thrive in group play.

Here are simple design considerations for inclusivity:

- **Solo → Pair → Group** progression respects varying comfort levels.
- Offer **written options** before discussion.
- Normalize **"pass" or "circle back"** as valid choices.
- Use **rotating roles** (note-taker, timekeeper, reporter) to diversify contributions.
- Don't confuse silence with disinterest—sometimes, it's depth.

Effective facilitation includes all voices, not by forcing expression, but by widening the invitation.

4. Prompt with Purpose

A mediocre question gets polite answers.
A powerful question **changes how people think**.

Crafting the right prompt is one of the facilitator's most strategic decisions. It's the difference between compliance and insight.

Ask:

- "What surprised you?" instead of "What did you learn?"
- "What might be missing?" instead of "Is this complete?"
- "What's the story behind that reaction?" instead of "Do you agree?"

The best prompts:

- Are open-ended and non-leading
- Connect to experience, not just opinion
- Create a bridge between the topic and the person

Want better answers? Ask better questions.

5. Energize Without Infantilizing

Engagement doesn't require games, glitter, or sticky notes shaped like stars. Adults don't need to be entertained. They need to feel *relevant*.

Use novelty strategically. Use play with purpose. But never condescend.

If you use a creative technique, tell people why:

"I'm using this metaphor tool because it helps us think beyond logic and into meaning."

Framing elevates even the simplest tool into an intentional act of learning design.

6. Endings Are Engagement, Too

Never close with: "Okay, that's it."
The way you **end** a session shapes how people **carry it forward**.

Powerful closings:

- Invite a final reflection or insight
- Return to the opening prompt or purpose
- Use a metaphor or story to land the message

- Offer time for personal action planning

Try:

- "What is one word to describe what you're leaving with?"
- "Write a headline for what today meant to you."
- "What's one conversation you want to have after this?"

A good close turns temporary engagement into **lasting integration**.

Real-Time Engagement Prompts

Here's a ready-to-use set of engagement starters categorized by purpose:

Purpose	Prompts
Open Space	"What's one word that captures where you are right now?"
Deepen Thinking	"What's a tension you're holding between X and Y?"
Connect Perspectives	"Whose voice or perspective is missing from this conversation?"
Build Meaning	"What insight are you sitting with that feels incomplete?"
Translate to Action	"What's one shift you'll try in your next interaction or meeting?"
Honor Emotion	"What surprised you emotionally about what we explored today?"

Your Turn

Closing: From Engagement Tactics to Transformational Presence

Designing engagement is not about filling time; it's about shaping experiences that matter.

The most impactful facilitators don't rely on charisma, cleverness, or control. They rely on presence, preparation, and purposeful prompts. They understand that engagement is not something we do to people, it's something we co-create with them.

At its core, engagement design is the art of building relevance, resonance, and relationships.

Whether you're facilitating a formal session or navigating a team meeting, a difficult conversation, or a community discussion, the SPARK IT! framework offers a compass for cultivating trust and momentum:

- **Set the Space** for clarity and emotional grounding.
- **Prompt with Purpose** to unlock reflection and insight.
- **Anchor in Context** so that learning feels lived-in, not abstract.
- **Respond with Curiosity** to signal respect and deepen exploration.
- **Kindle Connection** through empathy and inclusion.
- **Iterate in Real Time** to remain responsive to what emerges.

- **Translate Insight into Action** so that growth becomes movement.

These are not steps. They are moves. They are mindsets. They are choices you can make—moment by moment—to elevate engagement from a tactic to a transformative force.

Reflective Prompts: SPARK IT! in Action

S - Set the Space

- What signals (verbal, visual, tonal) am I using to communicate safety and purpose?
- How might I design the beginning of a meeting or conversation to feel more welcoming?

P - Prompt with Purpose

- What question could I ask that invites reflection rather than reaction?
- Am I choosing prompts that matter to this moment and this group?

A - Anchor in Context

- How can I connect this discussion to participants' real-life challenges or goals?
- Where might I be over-relying on theory instead of lived relevance?

R - Respond with Curiosity

- Am I listening to respond—or to truly understand?
- How do I make space for nuance and exploration instead of rushing to closure?

K - Kindle Connection

- What's one way I can help people see each other more fully today?
- How am I fostering empathy, not just interaction?

I - Iterate in Real Time

- What's happening in the room (or Zoom) right now that I need to respond to?
- Am I willing to let go of the script in service of what's alive?

T - Translate Insight into Action

- What will participants do, try, or see differently because of this engagement?
- How am I helping them connect insight to next steps?

Reflection Prompt: What Did it Feel Like?

Think about a time when you felt genuinely engaged during a group session. What made it work for you? What design choices do you remember?

Now, consider a time when you disengaged.

What happened-or didn't happen-that contributed to that feeling?

Everyday Practices for Engagement by Design

Try incorporating one or more of these habits into your daily facilitation, meetings, or conversations:

Begin with an Opening Prompt:
Start your next meeting by asking, "What's one thing you're carrying into this space today?" It immediately signals presence and shared humanity.

Design Quiet Think Time:
Build in 60-90 seconds of solo reflection before a group dialogue. This respects diverse processing styles and leads to deeper, more intentional contributions.

Use a Curiosity Reframe:
Instead of replying with "Why did you do that?", try, "Can you walk me through what was going on for you at that moment?" This subtle shift transforms interrogation into inquiry.

Signal Inclusion with Your Eyes and Voice:
Pause and ask, "Is there someone we haven't heard from who might see this differently?" And then hold space—silence is part of the design.

End with Meaning:
Close a discussion with a prompt like, "What's one idea or phrase that's staying with you?" or "What's one conversation this session inspired you to have?"

Reflect on Your Own Presence:
After any session or interaction, jot down:

- What engagement tactic worked well?
- What felt off or overused?
- Where did I respond or adapt in real time?

My Reflections

Chapter 8 in a Nutshell:
In Life & At Work

In Life:

At home and in your relationships, people aren't looking for perfection—they're looking for presence. Emotional infrastructure begins with empathy: the willingness to understand before being understood. When trust is present, people speak more honestly and listen more generously. You don't need advanced techniques; you need intentional curiosity. Ask more open questions. Practice pausing before responding. And remember, inclusion isn't about agreement—it's about respect. When people feel seen and safe, connection deepens.

At Work:

Workplaces run on more than processes—they run on emotional bandwidth. If your meetings feel performative or disengaged, it may be that trust hasn't been built or maintained. Facilitation is not just about directing conversation; it's about inviting courage. Use empathy as a leadership tool. Normalize vulnerability by being the first to acknowledge uncertainty or tension. Set psychological safety as a precondition, not a bonus. Inclusive dialogue is not a "nice to have"—it's the foundation for innovation, cohesion, and shared ownership.

ROBERT RADI

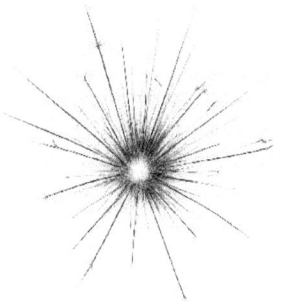

Chapter 9
Virtual Doesn't Mean Distant

When the world moved online, many feared that something vital would be lost: connection, nuance, and spontaneity. And in some cases, it was.

But virtual facilitation didn't invent distance. Poor facilitation did.

Distance isn't measured in pixels or Wi-Fi speed. It's measured in **presence**, **attention**, and **human design**. The best virtual facilitators don't recreate in-person sessions on a screen—they rethink how presence is built and sustained when people aren't physically together.

Facilitating virtually isn't just a technical skill. It's a **discipline of intentionality**. Every pause, question, visual, and tone of voice choice matters more because **the medium amplifies both friction and silence**.

This chapter is about turning the screen from a barrier into a bridge.

1. Start with Presence, Not Tech

The most common mistake in virtual facilitation is treating it as a content delivery vehicle. It's not. It's a **shared social moment**, with added constraints and new possibilities.

Presence can be created in subtle ways:

- Greet participants by name as they arrive
- Use *eye contact* (by looking into the camera)
- Acknowledge the humanity behind the screen: "Welcome—wherever you're joining from, however your day is going."

People don't log into your session to consume slides. They log in to feel included.

2. Design for Cognitive Load

Screens compress communication. We lose body language, ambient energy, and non-verbal cues. In their place, we get **Zoom fatigue**, reduced attention spans, and visual overstimulation. Virtual space rewards **simplicity + clarity + rhythm**.

To counter this:

- Reduce text. Amplify visuals and voice.
- Build in quiet. Don't fear silence; it allows integration.
- Change modalities every 10-15 minutes: discussion, chat, visuals, reflection.
- Use layout breaks: "We're going off video for 3 minutes to journal."

- Be explicit with transitions: "We're shifting now from insight to application."

3. Use the Tools, Don't Let Them Use You

Features like breakout rooms, polls, chats, and reactions aren't just bells and whistles. They're your virtual facilitation toolkit.

Use them strategically:

Tool	Purpose	Facilitation Tip
Chat	Low-barrier contribution, quiet voices	Prompt with clarity: "Type one word that…"
Breakouts	Psychological safety, intimacy, dialogue	Set structure: "One speaker, one notetaker."
Polls	Quick pulse checks, engagement sampling	Add a question: "What do you notice about this result?"
Reactions	Non-disruptive energy and consensus signals	Use thumbs up, red X, emojis for energy check
Screenshare	Anchor visuals, simplify complexity	Don't read slides— speak around them
Whiteboards	Collective brainstorming, co-creation	Limit tools: too many options create chaos

Remember: every tech choice is a design choice.

4. Curate the Environment for You and Them

Facilitators shape the room—even if it's digital. Before you facilitate:

- Clean your frame (what's visible on your camera)
- Check the lighting, background, and sound
- Minimize screen clutter and turn off notifications

But they also invite participants to do the same:

"If you can, find a space where you can focus. Bring a notebook. Give yourself permission to be here."

You can't control distractions, but you can **co-author the container.**

5. Address the Elephant: Zoom Fatigue

It's real. And it's not just about time on screen—it's about **how** time is spent.

Combat fatigue with:

- Rhythm: alternate intensity and rest
- Choice: allow "video off" time or breakout opt-outs
- Play: use music, visuals, surprise prompts
- Check-ins: ask, "How's your energy right now—1 to 5?"

Facilitators don't need to entertain. But they do need to **empathize with screen exhaustion**—and adjust accordingly.

6. Build Connection Without Proximity

In person, connection comes through eye contact, hallway chats, and shared physical space. Online, connection must be **consciously constructed**.

Try:

- First-name chats: "What's something you're bringing into the room today?"
- Virtual empathy: "Drop a word in chat that describes your current mindset."
- Paired breakouts: "Just talk. No agenda. Ask how they're really doing."
- Collaborative visuals: "On the whiteboard, draw how your week feels."

Connection doesn't happen by accident online. But it does occur, with care. Invite them to hold the space for each other and engage, explore, and enjoy each other's perspective.

7. Reframe Silence and Disruption

Facilitators may fear the dead air. However, silence on Zoom isn't always a sign of disengagement—it might be a reflection, a technical delay, or group processing.

Instead of panicking, name it:

"I notice we're sitting in some quiet right now. That's okay. Take a moment—what's coming up for you?"

And if tech fails, name that too:

"It seems we hit a glitch. That's part of being human in a digital world."

Graceful facilitation isn't about flawless delivery—it's about presence when things wobble.

8. Close with Intention

Virtual sessions can end abruptly. One minute, you're in dialogue; the next, you're looking at your email inbox.

So, slow the descent. Signal the transition.

Try:

- A closing chat prompt: "What's one idea you're walking away with?"
- A countdown visual: "2 minutes left—capture the next step."
- A farewell ritual: "Hold up a hand, send a thank-you emoji, or write a word of appreciation."

Closing well is a gift to your participants—and yourself.

Everyday Facilitation in a Virtual World

You don't need to run a workshop to facilitate meaningful online interactions. Every digital interaction—whether it's a Slack message, team huddle, one-on-one check-in, or family video call—is an opportunity to show up with presence and intention.

Consider:

- **Starting a weekly team call** by asking, "What's one win or challenge from this past week?"
- **Opening a family Zoom** with, "What's one moment you're grateful for today?"
- **Ending a virtual client meeting** with, "What's your next

step after this conversation?"

These aren't tricks. They're micro-moments of facilitation. You're holding space. You're sparking clarity. You're making remote connection feel real.

In a world where digital fatigue is the default, even a small gesture of intentional engagement can reset the emotional tone of a team or relationship.

Two Screens, Same Human Need

Team on a Screen

I once observed a team lead begin a virtual all-hands meeting by asking each member to type in one word describing their current energy. No discussion—just a silent cascade of words in the chat: *tired, hopeful, anxious, motivated, curious*. The leader paused, read each one aloud, and then said:

"Thanks for sharing that. It helps me know where we're starting from, not just what we need to cover."

In less than 90 seconds, the room shifted. People sat up. The meeting had a pulse. That wasn't just small talk—it was a signal. The leader had facilitated presence.

Family in Four Boxes

During the early days of the pandemic, a friend started hosting monthly Zoom dinners with her parents, siblings, and nieces. At first, it was chaotic: everyone talked over each other, and screen fatigue took its toll. Then one evening, she tried something different.
She sent a question in advance:

"What's a memory from our childhood that still makes you laugh?"

That night, each person shared one story. The youngest niece acted them out. The oldest sibling cried laughing. They ended the call feeling connected, not just updated.

That's facilitation, too.

SPARK IT! in Virtual Facilitation

The **SPARK IT!** framework isn't just for in-person settings. In fact, its power becomes even more evident when translated across digital platforms:

- **Set the Space** by welcoming people by name, acknowledging time zones, or grounding the moment with a quick check-in.

- **Prompt with Purpose** through concise, relevant chat questions or pre- and post-breakout reflections.

- **Anchor in Context** by sharing how today's topic connects to participants' current work, challenges, or goals—"Here's why this matters right now."

- **Respond with Curiosity** by embracing slower pacing, nonverbal cues, and unexpected input with presence.

- **Kindle Connection** by encouraging peer exchange, shared visual tools, or emotional prompts ("What color is your day today?").

- **Iterate in Real Time** by adjusting content pacing, extending conversations that are alive, or shifting formats to meet energy in the room.

- **Translate Insight into Action** with a final moment of reflection: "What's your first small step when we log off?"

In virtual facilitation, **SPARK IT!** is the compass.

Your Turn

Reflective Prompts for Virtual Facilitation Practice

Close the chapter with a set of journal-style reflections that let facilitators embed the learning:

- When was the last time you felt truly **present** in a virtual setting? What contributed to that moment?
- Which part of your current virtual facilitation could benefit from **simplification** or an intentional pause?
- How do you currently **signal transitions** in your virtual sessions? What could make them more fluid?
- What subtle practices help you **build connections** across screens?
- Which of the **SPARK IT!** principles do you want to experiment with in your next virtual meeting—and how?

My Reflections

Chapter 9 in a Nutshell:
In Life & At Work

In Life:

Distance is not just physical—it's emotional, relational, and intentional. Whether you're catching up with family over video chat or holding a virtual reunion with friends, presence matters more than tech. Look into the camera, speak from the heart, and create space for others to arrive fully. Connection online is not a weaker substitute—it's a different kind of opportunity. With care and creativity, a screen can become a window into someone's world, rather than a wall.

At Work:

Virtual facilitation isn't about replicating in-person sessions—it's about reimagining how we show up. Begin with human presence, not platform features. Greet people by name, reduce cognitive overload, and build rhythm into your sessions. Use the tools—breakouts, polls, visuals—with strategic simplicity, not as distractions. Most importantly, cultivate a sense of psychological presence. Your voice, tone, structure, and care are what hold the virtual room. Screens may separate us, but facilitation brings us back together.

ROBERT RADI

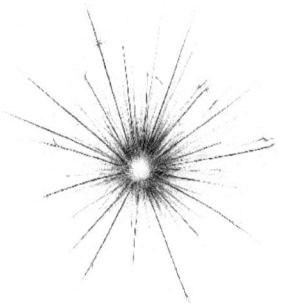

Chapter 10
Facilitation as a Lifelong Practice

By now, you've explored the mindset, the methods, and the moments. You've seen facilitation through the lenses of curiosity, courage, and connection. This chapter isn't a summary—it's a return and a reaching forward. A return to what has always made facilitation essential. A reaching forward into how you'll carry it with you next.

Some books aim to teach. Others to inspire. This one—if it has done its work—hopes to invite.
Not into a method, but into a mindset.
Not into a prescription, but into a practice.
Not into perfection, but into presence.

Facilitation, as we've explored throughout these pages, is not reserved for experts, executives, or educators. It's not confined to classrooms, boardrooms, or training sessions. It is a fundamentally ancient human act, necessary, and available to all of us.

The Dialogue Never Ends

As we have explored, the roots of facilitation stretch deep into history. Socrates didn't deliver lectures—he asked questions. He engaged in *maieutics*: the midwifing of wisdom through inquiry. He believed that truth and clarity arise not from declarations, but from shared dialogue.

Centuries later, psychologist Carl Rogers taught us that transformation occurs in environments of empathy, authenticity, and unconditional positive regard, not from authority, but from attuned presence. These aren't soft skills; they are conditions for psychological safety, self-discovery, and growth.

David Bohm, the theoretical physicist and philosopher, envisioned dialogue not as debate, but as a collective process of thinking together. In his words, "If we are to live in harmony with ourselves and with nature, we need to communicate."

Across cultures and traditions, people have formed circles around fires, altars, tables, and screens—not to assert dominance, but to make meaning together.

This is what we inherit when we choose to facilitate. And it's what we carry forward, one conversation at a time.

Vulnerability is Practice

At this point, you've encountered a wide range of tools, strategies, and models. But let's be honest: facilitation is not about mastering steps—it's about being willing to step in. Into uncertainty. Into silence. Into real human interaction.

Every time you ask a question that you don't have an answer to . . .

Every time you sit with silence rather than rushing to fill it . . . Every time you say, "I don't know, but let's find out together."

You are facilitating.

And yes, it can feel vulnerable. But vulnerability isn't weakness—it's the doorway to connection. As Brené Brown reminds us, "Vulnerability is the courage to show up and be seen when you can't control the outcome."

Your participants don't need you to be perfect. They need you to be present.

From Tools to Tuning

The SPARK IT! framework you've learned is not a formula—it's a compass. It helps you navigate the subtle, shifting terrain of group interaction.

Each component—**Set the Space, Prompt with Purpose, Anchor in Context, Respond with Curiosity, Kindle Connection, Iterate in Real Time,** and **Translate Insight into Action**—isn't something to check off, but something to attune to.

It's not about performance. It's about perception.

At your next family dinner, team check-in, or community forum, SPARK IT! might not appear on a flipchart, but it can quietly shape your presence. You might ask yourself:

- Is the space emotionally safe for people to speak their truth?
- Is my question surfacing what matters most now?
- Are we grounded in their reality or floating in abstraction?
- Am I listening to understand or just waiting to speak?
- What new insight is trying to emerge?

- Do I need to adapt based on what's unfolding?
- How can this moment lead to meaningful action?

This is where facilitation lives—not in events, but in *moments*.

The Courage to Begin (Again and Again)

There's no moment when you "arrive" as a facilitator. You begin. You try. You trip. You learn. You return—wiser, humbler, and more open.

Some sessions will fall flat. Some questions won't land. Some participants will resist. That's not failure—it's feedback. It's material.

Facilitation is not about having the answers. It's about being the kind of presence that welcomes the questions.

Let this be your permission slip:

- To begin before you feel ready.
- To create space even when silence feels risky.
- To let go of control and lean into curiosity.
- To practice—even when imperfect.

Because the next conversation could be the one that changes everything, for someone else, or you.

Facilitation as a Dynamic Orientation

Facilitation is not a static skill—it is a dynamic *orientation*. Like meditation, parenting, or leadership, it evolves. You grow with it. It grows with you.

1. From Doing to Becoming

Initially, you focus on "doing" facilitation: establishing the proper structure, managing time, and posing clear questions. But over time, facilitation becomes something you *are*, not just something you do. You start asking better questions in life, not just in sessions. You notice when others need space to speak. You hold tension without fixing it. You become a steward of possibility.

2. Returning to the Fundamentals

Mastery isn't about complication. It's about returning—again and again—to what matters.

- **Set the Space** no longer means arranging chairs. It means sensing emotional readiness.
- **Prompt with Purpose** shifts from clever questions to courageous ones.
- **Anchor in Context** is about helping people connect their truth to the conversation.
- **Respond with Curiosity** becomes your default when tension arises.
- **Kindle Connection** means creating the trust that holds complexity.
- **Iterate in Real Time** is what allows genuine responsiveness.
- **Translate Insight into Action** keeps the dialogue alive beyond the room.

3. When the Room Teaches You

Your most essential facilitation lessons won't come from books—they'll come from the room itself:

- A workshop that went off-script . . . but led to truth.
- A moment of silence that revealed something sacred.
- A difficult participant who reflected a part of you.

Facilitation teaches humility. You can plan meticulously—and still be surprised. And those surprises are where the learning lives.

4. Beyond the Workshop

Facilitation doesn't end when the meeting closes or the flipchart is capped. It lives in the hallway conversation. The hard feedback moment. The family dinner. The parenting dilemma.

You start noticing: Who's holding back? Who needs encouragement? What questions need space?

You begin asking yourself:
"What am I facilitating right now—confusion or clarity, tension or trust?"

Growth, Gaps, and Grace

The more you facilitate, the more you'll see your own patterns. Maybe you interrupt. Or over-explain. Or avoid conflict. These aren't flaws—they're feedback loops for your own development.

Lifelong facilitation requires the same grace for yourself that you offer others. Growth isn't linear. You will forget, remember, regress, and evolve. But you will always have another chance—to re-enter with more presence.

A Community of Practice

Facilitation is often a solo act—but development rarely happens alone.

Find others who care. Co-facilitate. Debrief. Get feedback. Read together. Reflect together. You don't just become better through experience—you become better through mirrors.

In a world of shallow connection and reactive discourse, your presence can be a calming force. You don't need a title—just the willingness to see and be seen.

From Skillset to Mindset

Facilitation is not a bag of tricks—it's a way of being. Tools matter, but tools without presence are just technique. Prompts without empathy are just performance.

Great facilitators are not the ones who speak the most, but the ones who listen the best.

In that sense, facilitation is not only about how you guide others; it is also about how you guide yourself. It's not just about conversations; it's about how you move through the world—with clarity, curiosity, humility, and care.

A Spiral, Not a Line

Facilitation is not a fixed skillset. It's a fluid, courageous way of walking with others. Let these questions return to you—again and again—not as checklists, but as tuning forks.

Your next opportunity to practice begins now.
Not at a retreat.
Not in a perfect room.
But right where you are.

The spark is yours.
Keep tending to it.

Shall we begin—again?

Your Turn

Reflective Practices

Here are a few prompts to sustain your facilitation journey long after the final page:

Presence
- When do I feel most present in a conversation? What helps me arrive fully?
- What distracts me from really listening—and how might I gently return?

Curiosity
- What question have I not dared to ask recently?
- How can I bring more wonder and less judgment into my daily interactions?

Connection
- Who in my life needs to feel more seen or heard right now?
- What's one small gesture I can make to build trust?

Courage
- Where am I hesitating to speak or lead? What story might I be telling myself?
- What does "brave facilitation" look like in my current context?

Growth
- What did I learn from a recent facilitation moment—good or bad?
- What one slight shift could elevate how I design or hold space?

Your next conversation starts now. Not on a stage. Not at a retreat. But here, in the everyday.

My Reflections

Chapter 10 in a Nutshell:
In Life & At Work

In Life:

Facilitation is not limited to meeting rooms or structured sessions—it's a mindset of presence, curiosity, and compassion that applies to everyday interactions. At the dinner table, in difficult conversations, or during moments of uncertainty, facilitation becomes a form of quiet leadership. By listening deeply, asking purposefully, and holding space for others to think, you help people feel seen and heard. This chapter reminds us that our presence—more than our perfection—makes the difference.

At Work:

Great facilitators aren't born—they are shaped through practice, reflection, and humility. In a fast-changing workplace, facilitation becomes a strategic asset: helping teams navigate ambiguity, foster trust, and unlock shared intelligence. The SPARK IT! framework isn't a checklist—it's a compass. Use it to refine your craft in meetings, projects, and everyday engagements. And remember, facilitation is never finished. It evolves with you, and with the courage to keep showing up, as do your outcomes.

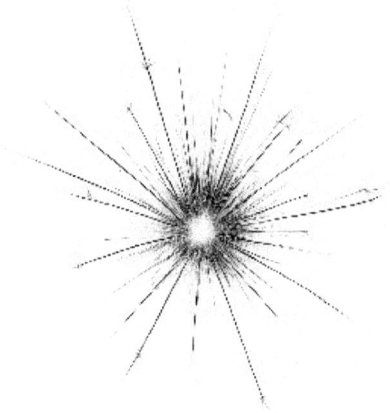

Conclusion
Sustain and Protect the SPARK

Facilitation is more than a skill. It's a way of showing up—in conversation, in conflict, in community. It's how we move from telling to listening, from managing to meaning-making, from performing to being present.

By now, you've explored mindsets and methods. You've met the SPARK IT! framework—not as a formula, but as a fluid guide to shaping conversations with care, purpose, and adaptability.

You've heard stories, practiced prompts, and reflected on what it means to create conditions where others feel safe to think, feel, and grow. But the real work begins after the final page.

The Book Wasn't the Goal—You Are

This book isn't an endpoint. It's an aperture. A portal into the lifelong art of inviting others into clarity, dignity, and contribution. If you feel inspired, unsure, or even a little daunted—good. That means the work is alive in you.
Don't wait to feel "ready." The world is filled with meetings that need meaning, conversations that need care, and people who are longing to be heard.
You can be that space. You already are.

Facilitation Is an Act of Hope

In every room you enter—virtual or in person—you carry an unseen offer: the chance to listen more deeply, ask more generously, and respond with greater humanity. That's not soft. That's transformative.
To facilitate is to believe in people's capacity to co-create. It is to hold complexity with composure. It is to trust that dialogue can move what data alone cannot.
It doesn't require a whiteboard or a title—just a willingness to be present in the places where insight waits to emerge.

Your Imperfection Is an Asset

You don't have to be the most articulate person in the room. You don't need flawless timing or perfect confidence. In fact, the best facilitators are often the most humble ones—the ones who know how to pause, pivot, apologize, and begin again.

Every moment of uncertainty is a chance to practice.

Every failed session is a seed of wisdom.

Every awkward silence is an invitation to listen more fully.

You Are Not Alone

Facilitation may feel solitary at times, but you are joining a lineage of teachers, mentors, community leaders, conflict mediators, and kitchen-table gatherers who have shaped spaces of insight and healing for generations. You are now part of that tradition.
And you don't have to walk it alone. Seek out your circle–trade stories. Ask for feedback. Show your process. You're not building a brand–you're building a practice. And practice thrives in community.

Carry the Spark Forward

So, what now?
Now, you take the spark–whatever it looks like for you–and carry it into your next moment of presence. Into your team call. Into your family conversation. Into that tough meeting you've been dreading. Into the spaces that matter most to you.
You don't need to perform facilitation. You just need to practice it. One thoughtful question. One pause. One deep breath. One step closer to a real connection.
Because the world doesn't just need more communication.
It needs more communion.
And it needs you, not as an expert, but as someone brave enough to hold space when it counts.
Thank you for showing up. Now go–spark something.

A Final Encouragement

You don't need to be perfect. You don't need to wait for a certificate. You only need to begin.

To open the next conversation.

To stay with the next silence.

To ask the next question that matters.

To light the next spark.

Because the world doesn't just need more experts.
It needs more facilitators.

It needs you.

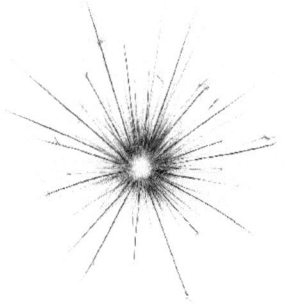

Acknowledgments

Semper Gratus

There is no greater deception than believing we are self-made. Our personal and professional journeys are intricately woven through moments of connection, guidance, and collaboration.

Semper Gratus—always grateful—is more than a Latin phrase. It is a guiding principle I strive to live by. I stand here as a testament to the profound impact of the many individuals who have contributed to my path.

I extend my deepest gratitude to my family. Your unwavering support, love, and patience have been the bedrock of my resilience. To my wife, Charlotte, your wisdom and insight continue to be a source of strength and clarity. Thank you for being the compass that steadies my course.

To my colleagues and mentors, past and present, your guidance has shaped my professional ethos and sharpened my strategic lens. To the mentors who generously shared their experience and perspective, your influence on my thinking and trajectory is beyond measure.

To my peer review group, thank you for your critical insights and honest feedback. Your diverse perspectives and thoughtful critiques elevated this book in ways I could not have achieved on my own.

To my friends, thank you for your encouragement, patience, and the countless hours spent in discussion and reflection. Your presence has been a constant source of joy, growth, and perspective.

To the thinkers and scholars whose work has inspired mine, especially those whose strategic frameworks have shaped my own, your intellectual contributions continue to challenge, guide, and broaden my perspective on what is possible.

And to you, the reader, thank you for choosing to embark on this journey. Your curiosity brings these pages to life. I hope this book becomes a trusted companion on your path toward clarity, intentionality, and self-authorship.

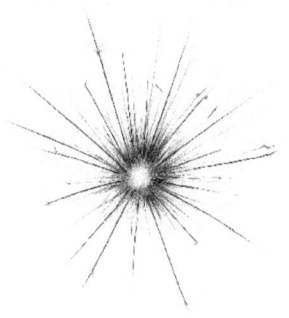

Bibliography

Chapter 1 - SPARK IT! A Framework for Human-Centered Facilitation

Aristotle. (2007). *On rhetoric: A theory of civic discourse* (G. A. Kennedy, Trans.). Oxford University Press. (Original work published ca. 4th century BCE)

Bandura, A. (1977). *Social learning theory*. Prentice-Hall.

Dewey, J. (1938). *Experience and education*. Kappa Delta Pi.

Diamond, A. (2013). Executive functions. *Annual Review of Psychology*, 64, 135–168. https://doi.org/10.1146/annurev-psych-113011-143750

Radi, R. (2023). *Inception mindset: The art and science of leading in a permanently complex world*. LHH Publishing.

Vygotsky, L. S. (1978). *Mind in society: The development of higher psychological processes*. Harvard University Press.

Chapter 2 - Socratic Presence: Asking Over Telling

Christensen, C. M., Allworth, J., & Dillon, K. (2012). *How will you measure your life?* Harper Business.

Lipman, M. (2003). *Thinking in education* (2nd ed.). Cambridge University Press.

Paul, R., & Elder, L. (2006). *The miniature guide to the art of asking essential questions*. Foundation for Critical Thinking.

Radi, R. (2023). *Inception mindset: The art and science of leading in a permanently complex world*. LHH Publishing.

Senge, P. M. (1990). *The fifth discipline: The art and practice of the learning organization*. Doubleday.

Socrates. (2002). *The trial and death of Socrates* (G. M. A. Grube, Trans.; 3rd ed.). Hackett Publishing Company. (Original work published ca. 399 BCE)

Chapter 3 - Facilitating Learning: Training or Development?

Argyris, C., & Schön, D. A. (1974). *Theory in practice: Increasing professional effectiveness*. Jossey-Bass.

Dewey, J. (1938). *Experience and education*. Kappa Delta Pi.

Freire, P. (1970). *Pedagogy of the oppressed*. Herder and Herder.

Knowles, M. S., Holton, E. F., & Swanson, R. A. (2015). *The adult learner: The definitive classic in adult education and human resource development* (8th ed.). Routledge.

Kolb, D. A. (1984). *Experiential learning: Experience as the source of learning and development*. Prentice-Hall.

Radi, R. (2023). *Inception mindset: The art and science of leading in a permanently complex world*. LHH Publishing.

Chapter 4 - Crafting Your Facilitation Philosophy

Argyris, C., & Schön, D. A. (1974). *Theory in practice: Increasing professional effectiveness*. Jossey-Bass.

Brookfield, S. D. (1995). *Becoming a critically reflective teacher*. Jossey-Bass.

Freire, P. (1970). *Pedagogy of the oppressed*. Herder and Herder.

Kegan, R., & Lahey, L. L. (2009). *Immunity to change: How to overcome it and unlock potential in yourself and your organization*. Harvard Business Press.

Palmer, P. J. (1998). *The courage to teach: Exploring the inner landscape of a teacher's life*. Jossey-Bass.

Petrie, N. (2014). *Vertical development: The next big thing in leadership development?* Center for Creative Leadership.

Radi, R. (2023). *Inception mindset: The art and science of leading in a permanently complex world*. LHH Publishing.

Vygotsky, L. S. (1978). *Mind in society: The development of higher psychological processes*. Harvard University Press.

Chapter 5 - Stories That Spark: Facilitating Meaning Through Narrative

Bruner, J. (1990). *Acts of meaning*. Harvard University Press.

Denning, S. (2005). *The leader's guide to storytelling: Mastering the art and discipline of business narrative*. Jossey-Bass.

Gottschall, J. (2012). *The storytelling animal: How stories make us human*. Houghton Mifflin Harcourt.

Heath, C., & Heath, D. (2007). *Made to stick: Why some ideas survive and others die*. Random House.

Radi, R. (2015). *The process of political narrative construct: How political leaders construct new narratives while experiencing adverse political conditions* (Doctoral dissertation, The Chicago School of Professional Psychology).

Radi, R. (2023). *Inception mindset: The art and science of leading in a permanently complex world*. LHH Publishing.

Chapter 6 - The Courage to Adjust: Responsive Facilitation

Argyris, C., & Schön, D. A. (1978). *Organizational learning: A theory of action perspective*. Addison-Wesley.

Brookfield, S. D. (2017). *Becoming a critically reflective teacher* (2nd ed.). Jossey-Bass.

Heifetz, R. A., Grashow, A., & Linsky, M. (2009). *The practice of adaptive leadership: Tools and tactics for changing your organization and the world*. Harvard Business Press.

Radi, R. (2015). *The process of political narrative construct: How political leaders construct new narratives while experiencing adverse political conditions* (Doctoral dissertation, The Chicago School of Professional Psychology).

Radi, R. (2023). *Inception mindset: The art and science of leading in a permanently complex world*. LHH Publishing.

Schon, D. A. (1983). *The reflective practitioner: How professionals think in action*. Basic Books.

Chapter 7 - Building the Emotional Infrastructure: Trust, Empathy, and Inclusive Dialogue

Brown, B. (2018). *Dare to lead: Brave work. Tough conversations. Whole hearts.* Random House.

Covey, S. M. R. (2006). *The speed of trust: The one thing that changes everything.* Free Press.

Goleman, D. (1995). *Emotional intelligence: Why it can matter more than IQ.* Bantam Books.

Rogers, C. R. (1961). *On becoming a person: A therapist's view of psychotherapy.* Houghton Mifflin.

Radi, R. (2023). *Inception mindset: The art and science of leading in a permanently complex world.* LHH Publishing.

Chapter 8 - Engagement Design: Tools, Prompts, and Tactics

Brookfield, S. D., & Preskill, S. (2005). *Discussion as a way of teaching: Tools and techniques for democratic classrooms* (2nd ed.). Jossey-Bass.

Brown, B. (2018). *Dare to lead: Brave work. Tough conversations. Whole hearts.* Random House.

Duarte, N. (2012). *Resonate: Present visual stories that transform audiences.* Wiley.

Kegan, R., & Lahey, L. L. (2009). *Immunity to change: How to overcome it and unlock potential in yourself and your organization.* Harvard Business Press.

Kolb, D. A. (1984). *Experiential learning: Experience as the source of learning and development.* Prentice Hall.

Radi, R. (2023). *Inception mindset: The art and science of leading in a permanently complex world.* LHH Publishing.

Wheatley, M. (2002). *Turning to one another: Simple conversations to restore hope to the future.* Berrett-Koehler.

Chapter 9 – Virtual Doesn't Mean Distant

Cascio, W. F., & Montealegre, R. (2016). How technology is changing work and organizations. *Annual Review of Organizational Psychology and Organizational Behavior,* 3(1), 349–375. https://doi.org/10.1146/annurev-orgpsych-041015-062352

Goleman, D. (2006). *Social intelligence: The new science of human relationships.* Bantam Books.

Mehrabian, A. (1971). *Silent messages.* Wadsworth Publishing.

Morgan, J. (2020). *The future leader: 9 skills and mindsets to succeed in the next decade.* Wiley.

Radi, R. (2023). *Inception mindset: The art and science of leading in a permanently complex world.* LHH Publishing.

Schein, E. H. (2013). *Humble inquiry: The gentle art of asking instead of telling.* Berrett-Koehler.

Turkle, S. (2015). *Reclaiming conversation: The power of talk in a digital age.* Penguin Books.

Chapter 10 – Facilitation as a Lifelong Practice

Bruner, J. (1990). *Acts of meaning.* Harvard University Press.

Damasio, A. (1999). *The feeling of what happens: Body and emotion in the making of consciousness.* Harcourt Brace.

Dweck, C. S. (2006). *Mindset: The new psychology of success.* Random House.

Elliott, R., Bohart, A. C., Watson, J. C., & Greenberg, L. S. (2011). *Empathy*. American Psychological Association. https://doi.org/10.1037/12327-000

Maslow, A. H. (1943). A theory of human motivation. *Psychological Review*, 50(4), 370–396. https://doi.org/10.1037/h0054346

Radi, R. (2023). *Inception mindset: The art and science of leading in a permanently complex world*. LHH Publishing.

Ricoeur, P. (1992). *Oneself as another* (K. Blamey, Trans.). University of Chicago Press.

Rogers, C. R. (1961). *On becoming a person: A therapist's view of psychotherapy*. Houghton Mifflin.

Schön, D. A. (1983). *The reflective practitioner: How professionals think in action*. Basic Books.

Wheatley, M. J. (2002). *Turning to one another: Simple conversations to restore hope to the future*. Berrett-Koehler.

Index

Abraham Lincoln ... 34
Abstract ... 3, 8, 14, 33, 35, 36, 38, 49, 58
Adele Diamond ... 11
Amy Edmondson ... 48
Anchor in Context ... 3, 8, 9, 13, 20, 58, 65, 68, 69
Andy Vossler ... 7
Carl Rogers ... 67
Cognitive ... 7, 9, 11, 20, 48, 49, 52, 62, 66
Collaboration ... 3, 7, 10, 33, 43, 53, 55, 74
Community ... 5, 7, 8, 23, 32, 35, 39, 55, 58, 68, 69, 71, 72
Complex ... 3, 4, 8, 18, 21, 22, 34, 38, 75, 76, 77, 78, 79, 80
Complexity ... 7, 10, 16, 20, 23, 27, 33, 69, 72
Content ... 8, 14, 16, 20, 21, 22, 23, 24, 27, 29, 33, 39, 40
Context ... 3, 8, 9, 12, 13, 14, 20, 22, 37, 53, 58, 65, 68, 69, 71
Creating ... 6, 12, 13, 16, 20, 21, 22, 31, 34, 47, 69
David Bohm ... 67
David Eagleman ... 31
Design ... 14, 18, 49, 50, 51, 52, 55, 56, 57, 58, 59, 62, 71, 78
Development ... 2, 7, 11, 20, 21, 22, 23, 24, 25, 29, 30, 69, 70
Discovery ... 6, 15, 16, 19, 28, 55, 67
Effective ... 4, 6, 14, 15, 16, 31, 33, 35, 40, 46, 51, 55, 56
Emotion ... 11, 35, 36, 37, 41, 49, 50, 80
Empathy ... 3, 9, 10, 13, 22, 32, 46, 47, 48, 49, 55, 58, 59, 60
Engagement ... 7, 11, 39, 48, 55, 56, 57, 58, 59, 64, 78
Experience ... 8, 15, 21, 27, 28, 29, 32, 33, 35, 37, 39, 40, 42, 51
Exploration ... 7, 9, 10, 16, 56, 58, 59
Facilitating ... 1, 3, 5, 7, 15, 20, 24, 28, 29, 31, 37, 40, 43, 47, 49, 51
Family ... 3, 8, 14, 35, 47, 64, 66, 68, 69, 73, 74
Growth ... 10, 13, 23, 25, 27, 28, 29, 30, 34, 35, 41, 42, 49, 58
Guiding ... 3, 10, 21, 31, 35, 74
Humility ... 16, 27, 41, 69, 70, 71
Inclusive ... 46, 50, 51, 52, 55, 60, 78
Inquiry ... 3, 6, 9, 15, 16, 17, 18, 19, 45, 47, 56, 59, 67, 79
Intentional ... 3, 5, 9, 10, 14, 18, 33, 42, 55, 56, 57, 59, 60, 64, 65, 66
Interactions ... 1, 3, 4, 6, 14, 20, 47, 64, 70, 71

Iterate in Real Time ... 3, 11, 12, 13, 22, 27, 47, 58, 59, 65, 68, 69
Kindle Connection ... 3, 10, 11, 13, 47, 54, 58, 59, 65, 68, 69
Leadership ... 2, 7, 8, 9, 12, 14, 15, 16, 17, 21, 23, 24
Meaningful ... 1, 3, 4, 7, 12, 13, 14, 17, 18, 35, 39, 40, 56, 64, 68
Meg Wheatley ... 39
Narrative ... 31, 32, 34, 35, 36, 37, 38, 40, 77, 78
Neuroscience ... 7, 8, 9, 10, 11, 32, 49
Organization ... 8, 23, 76, 78, 79, 83
Paul Zak ... 32
Perspective ... 10, 17, 20, 29, 33, 37, 63, 74, 75, 77
Philosophy ... 6, 16, 26, 27, 28, 29, 35, 76
Planning ... 12, 13, 14, 31, 52, 57
President Barack Obama ... 34
Prompt with Purpose ... 3, 6, 7, 8, 13, 56, 58, 65, 68, 69
Relationships ... 2, 10, 19, 23, 32, 45, 55, 58, 60, 79
Resistance ... 11, 27, 42, 43, 45, 48, 54
Respect ... 10, 27, 47, 48, 55, 58, 60
Respond with Curiosity ... 3, 9, 10, 13, 14, 47, 54, 58, 65, 68, 69
Set the Space ... 3, 5, 6, 13, 14, 23, 47, 54, 58, 65, 68, 69
Storytelling ... 8, 10, 31, 32, 34, 36, 38, 77
Structure ... 5, 17, 21, 22, 28, 32, 36, 39, 43, 66, 69
Teams ... 5, 18, 19, 22, 38, 45, 71
Thinking ... 9, 15, 16, 17, 18, 19, 20, 21, 34, 40, 54, 67, 74, 76
Tina Fey ... 34
Transformation ... 3, 20, 21, 22, 23, 24, 31, 35, 46, 67
Translate Insight into Action ... 3, 12, 13, 58, 59, 65, 68, 69
Trust ... 3, 4, 8, 10, 12, 14, 19, 22, 24, 27, 29, 32, 34, 35, 41, 42, 45, 46, 47
Values ... 25, 27, 28, 29, 31, 32, 38, 43, 50
Verbal ... 39, 43, 49, 51, 52, 58, 62
Virtual ... 51, 52, 62, 63, 64, 65, 66, 72, 79
Visual ... 52, 58, 62, 64, 65, 79
Voice ... 5, 12, 14, 16, 28, 47, 48, 52, 55, 59, 62, 66
Vulnerability ... 10, 32, 33, 37, 38, 42, 49, 55, 60, 67, 68
Wisdom ... 4, 9, 15, 16, 21, 22, 27, 29, 45, 67, 72, 74

About the Author

Dr. Robert Radi is the president and a partner at **Integral Advantage®**, an accredited organization committed to developing leadership capacity and strategic effectiveness across private, public, and nonprofit sectors. With more than three decades of multifaceted experience in domestic and international markets, Dr. Radi brings a rare combination of executive insight, entrepreneurial acumen, academic rigor, and public service to his work.

A seasoned executive, educator, and former elected official, Dr. Radi holds a Ph.D. in Organizational Leadership from The Chicago School and an MBA from Pepperdine University. He has served in various executive and board capacities across corporate, academic, nonprofit, and government institutions. Before his work in executive education and leadership development, he founded a consumer product strategy firm that supported global brands, led the development of iconic product platforms generating over $100 million in annual revenue, secured multiple patents, and earned numerous awards for innovation excellence.

As an educator, Dr. Radi has collaborated with institutions including The Chicago School, Pepperdine University, Benedictine University, University of Maryland, and California State University San Bernardino – Palm Desert Campus. He has taught at the bachelor's, master's, and doctoral levels, designing courses and frameworks that integrate executive leadership, strategic management, and organizational development.

Within the U.S. Federal Government, Dr. Radi is a sought-after subject matter expert and facilitator. He has delivered high-impact courses and keynote lectures to leaders and emerging professionals across federal agencies and the U.S. military, earning consistent acclaim for his clarity, relevance, and depth.

In civic leadership, he served two terms as a Council Member for the City of La Quinta, where he also chaired the boards of **SunLine Transit Agency** and the **Coachella Valley Association of Governments' Transportation Committee**. His public service resulted in measurable improvements in public safety, infrastructure, and economic development.

Known as a *pragmatic constructivist*, Dr. Radi's first book, *Inception Mindset*, has been widely recognized with numerous honors, including:

- 2024 **NYC Big Book Award** – Distinguished Favorite

- 2024 **International Impact Book Award** – Winner, Management

- Two 2024 **Independent Press Awards** – Distinguished Favorites in Leadership and Business: Entrepreneurship & Small Business

- Two **BookFest Spring 2024 Awards** – Business Leadership: Leadership & Management and Psychology & Mindset

- **International Book Awards 2024** – Finalist, Business: Entrepreneurship & Small Business

- A 5-star editorial review from **Reader Views**, calling it *"An Elucidating Masterpiece."*

Inception Mindset is available in print, eBook, and audiobook formats.

Follow the QR code for more information.

Follow the QR code for more information about Integral Advantage.

Integral Advantage® is a woman- and minority-owned leadership development firm dedicated to transforming how individuals and organizations think, lead, and perform. With a national footprint and a reputation for excellence across public, private, and nonprofit sectors, Integral Advantage® specializes in delivering high-impact, experiential learning rooted in strategic thinking, human-centered design, and behavioral science. The firm's signature frameworks—such as Entrusted Empowerment® and CADE™—equip leaders at all levels to navigate complexity, spark alignment, and drive sustainable outcomes. As an **IACET-accredited provider**, Integral Advantage® offers CEU-qualified programs that meet the highest standards of instructional design, evaluation, and effectiveness.

About inPrime Articles

Follow the QR code for more information about our inPrime Articles.

Our *inPrime Articles* are always free and always insightful, crafted to provoke thought, spark learning, and drive real-world implementation. Whether you're navigating a leadership challenge, facilitating a critical conversation, or simply seeking clarity in complex situations, these concise reads deliver practical wisdom and fresh perspectives—no paywall, no fluff—just high-impact ideas you can use today.

You can read or listen to each article.

www.ingramcontent.com/pod-product-compliance
Lightning Source LLC
Chambersburg PA
CBHW060503030426
42337CB00015B/1719